I0461545

© 2025 Frater Lachesis Peyton

Published by Saklas Publishing

ISBN: 979-8-9943016-6-1
First Edition
Printed in the United States of America

What This Book Is

This work is a magical record of my engagement with Liber LXV, Chapter III, combining personal vision, technical analysis, and contextual reflection on the A∴A∴ system. It documents what happened when I followed the published A∴A∴ instructions as I understood them: memorize, saturate, analyze, record, and examine. The process spanned nine years of recitation, verse-by-verse scansion, numerical reduction, and correspondence work. The result is a horizontal reading of the chapter—a man walking to execution, a woman already dead, a seal broken between worlds—that emerged alongside the traditional vertical reading of aspirant and Angel. Both interpretations coexist within the same textual architecture. I offer this as one path, one cosmology, one reading, not as a replacement or final word.

What This Book Is Not

This is not an official A∴A∴ document, not a definitive commentary, and not an attempt to close interpretation. I do not claim institutional authority within the A∴A∴ I write as a practitioner who followed the published instructions and documented the outcomes. The interpretive conclusions are mine. The structural findings—stress counts, numerical reductions, correspondences—are reproducible; readers may confirm, modify, or reject them based on their own engagement.

Method in Brief

The five-stage process I applied:

1. **Memorization** - Commit the text to exact internal recall without paraphrase

2. **Saturation** - Sustained recitation over years until the text becomes structurally embedded
3. **Analysis** - Apply scansion, gematria, Liber 777 correspondences, and Tarot attribution
4. **Recording** - Document findings systematically in written form
5. **Examination** - Test outcomes against the text and the tradition

This is the method Crowley described as Scientific Illuminism. It treats texts as operational rather than devotional. The goal is not belief but demonstrable engagement with structured symbolic material. Results follow from sustained attention, not from metaphysical claims.

TABLE OF CONTENTS

A∴A∴

Argentum Astrum

-

Astron Argon

FOLLOW the

SILVER STAR

Frater Lachesis Peyton

CHAPTER ONE
THE STRUCTURE SPEAKS

Liber LXV Chapter III – A Verse-by-Verse Analysis

Chapter III of Liber Cordis Cincti Serpente contains 65 verses and is attributed to the Element of Water within the A∴A∴ system (Crowley, 1910). The number 65 corresponds to the Hebrew אדני (Adonai), meaning "Lord", the name traditionally associated with the Holy Guardian Angel in this tradition.

The traditional interpretation frames this chapter as a dialogue between the Aspirant and the Holy Guardian Angel. The soul reaches upward; the Angel reaches down. Union is sought, achieved, lost, sought again.

This reading is supported by the text itself, by Crowley's own commentaries, and by the broader A∴A∴ curriculum in which the Knowledge and Conversation of the Holy Guardian Angel is the central attainment of the Adept grades. I do not dispute this reading. It served me for years. But after the chapter stabilized in my memory, after the words ceased to be something I retrieved and became something I simply was, a second reading emerged for me.

In this reading, the Angel and the Aspirant are not two. They are one, separated only by death. The voice speaking in Chapter III is not an Aspirant calling out to a distant Angel. It is the Angel speaking, looking back at the final day of the life that made him. The Aspirant does not seek the Angel. The Aspirant becomes the

Angel, through a specific event, and the Angel now narrates that becoming.

The event is an execution.

The speaker is a man walking to the gallows. His beloved, a woman the Church called "witch", has already been killed. He watched it happen. Now it is his turn. And the chapter traces that walk: the approach, the ascent, the platform, the drop, the death, and the rising. The traditional reading is vertical — Aspirant below, Angel above, reaching toward union. My reading is horizontal — a man walking forward through time toward a fixed point, and what happens when he reaches it. Both may be true.

∴

A Note on Method

Crowley states in his essay on Gematria that the magician performs countless calculations until the mind is ready to receive the flash of truth (Crowley, 1912). The calculations themselves are not the point. The process is the point — the disciplined attention, the pattern-seeking, the saturation of consciousness with symbolic material until something clicks.

I have applied the method to all 65 verses. The stress counts vary — some verses carry 4, some 5, some 6, some more. When those counts are mapped sequentially across the chapter, a wave pattern emerges. I will present that pattern visually in a later section.

I do not show the work for every verse. I am showing my method. The tables contain the complete data — every stress count, every reduction, every correspondence. The calculations are there.

What matters is not the mechanical process, but what the process revealed.

∴

The Verses

Verse 1

"Verily and Amen! I passed through the deep sea, and by the rivers of running water that abound therein, and I came unto the Land of No Desire." (Crowley, 1910, III:1)

Scansion

To analyze the meter, I spoke this verse internally, as I had thousands of times over nine years, and marked where the natural stresses fell. The method is simple: speak the line as you would speak it — not theatrically, not with imposed rhythm, but naturally. The stresses reveal themselves.

First clause: "Verily and Amen! I passed through the deep sea" Primary stresses: VER-, MEN, PASSED, DEEP, SEA — Count: 5

Second clause: "and by the rivers of running water that abound therein, and I came unto the Land of No Desire" Primary stresses: RIV-, RUN-, BOUND, CAME, LAND, SIRE — Count: 6

The Numbers

5 + 6 = 11

In the Qabalistic system documented in Liber 777 (Crowley, 1909), the number 11 carries specific significance: it is the number of Magick itself, the Great Work. 11 = 5 + 6 = Pentagram + Hexagram = Microcosm + Macrocosm = Man + God. It is also the number of the Qliphoth, the "shells" or adverse forces — that which must be crossed.

The verse does not approximate this structure. In my analysis, it is this structure. The content speaks of passage — "I passed through the deep sea." The form encodes the number of that passage.

The Image

"The deep sea" and "rivers of running water" — the speaker is traveling through something. Not standing still. Not contemplating. Moving.

"The Land of No Desire" — this phrase arrested me. In mystical literature, the cessation of desire is often framed as attainment, as peace, as liberation. But there is another state in which desire ceases: resignation. The condemned man no longer desires escape. He has accepted what is coming.

A man walking. Moving through water — perhaps literally, perhaps crossing a river, perhaps the rain, perhaps his own tears. Arriving at a place where desire has stopped, not because he has transcended it, but because he knows what awaits him.

This is the first step.

∴

Verse 2

"Wherein was a white unicorn with a silver collar, whereon was graven the aphorism Linea viridis gyrat universa." (Crowley, 1910, III:2)

4

The Image

The traditional interpretation reads the unicorn as a symbol of purity, singularity, and the unattainable. The silver collar suggests consecration or binding to divine purpose. The Latin aphorism — "The green line circles the universe" — is typically associated with Hermetic symbolism: the Emerald Tablet, the ouroboros, cyclical totality.

That reading is coherent within established symbolic frameworks.

In my reading, the image resolves differently.

"A white unicorn" — white, singular, upward-pointing. In this interpretive frame, the conical image suggests the pointed hat associated with accused witches. The shape is not treated as a mythical beast, but as a visible marker. The brightness draws attention. The symbol becomes embodied.

"With a silver collar" — something encircling the neck. A band. A ring. In this reading, the collar corresponds to a rope. Silver because it catches light. A collar because it encircles the throat. The image anticipates binding.

"Linea viridis gyrat universa" — "The green line circles the universe." Green. Line. Circle. Closure.

For a condemned man whose beloved has been executed, the rope becomes totalizing. The line defines the boundary of experience. The world narrows to a loop.

The aphorism, read this way, does not function as cosmology. It describes enclosure.

The Numbers

The scansion yields approximately 5 primary stresses in the English line, with the Latin phrase carrying approximately 4.

$5 + 4 = 9$

In Liber 777, 9 corresponds to:

- Yesod, the Foundation
- The Moon — reflection, image, illusion
- The grade of Zelator ($2°=9°$)

Nine is structurally foundational. Within this reading, the image of binding establishes the base condition of the narrative: the woman, the instrument, the event that follows.

The image is singular. The interpretation is layered. The structure remains intact.

∴

Verse 3

"Then the word of Adonai came unto me by the mouth of the Magister mine, saying: O heart that art girt about with the coils of the old serpent, lift up thyself unto the mountain of initiation!" (Crowley, 1910, III:3)

The Image

The traditional reading identifies Adonai as the Holy Guardian Angel speaking through the Magister, calling the aspirant toward initiation.

In the alternate reading, the phrase "by the mouth of the Magister mine" carries institutional weight. "Magister" can denote teacher or authority. In a historical context of condemnation, it can also denote the authority administering judgment.

The phrase "the word of Adonai" becomes ambiguous. "Lord" can refer to the Angel within Thelemic symbolism, but it also carries ecclesiastical resonance.

"O heart that art girt about with the coils of the old serpent" introduces multiple symbolic layers. In Gnostic traditions, the serpent can represent wisdom; in orthodox Christian inversion, it represents corruption. The coil can also describe a noose.

"Lift up thyself unto the mountain of initiation" traditionally suggests ascent. In the horizontal reading, the "mountain" may correspond to the raised platform of execution. The language of elevation intersects with the mechanics of death.

The irony is structural. The language of initiation overlays the language of condemnation. Whether intended or not, the symbolic system permits both readings simultaneously.

∴

Verse 4

"But I remembered. Yea, Than, yea, Theli, yea, Lilith! these three were about me from of old. For they are one." (Crowley, 1910, III:4)

The Image

Than, Theli, and Lilith each carry established symbolic associations.

- Than — death, serpent imagery, Leviathanic resonance
- Theli — the dragon or axis referenced in Sepher Yetzirah
- Lilith — the independent feminine figure of later myth

The verse asserts not merely proximity but continuity: "about me from of old." The three are declared one.

Triadic structures recur across symbolic systems: fate, birth-life-death cycles, triple goddesses, triune principles. The interpretive field is broad.

Within the execution narrative reading, the triad can be mapped onto inevitability — forces present from the beginning, converging at the end. The declaration "they are one" collapses multiplicity into unity.

The condemned figure does not describe surprise. He describes recognition.

The structure of the verse asserts that what appears as three resolves as one. The numerical and symbolic compression is explicit in the text itself.

∴

Verses 5-7

"Beautiful wast thou, O Lilith, thou serpent-woman!

Thou wast lithe and delicious to the taste, and thy perfume was of musk mingled with ambergris.

Close didst thou cling with thy coils unto the heart, and it was as the joy of all the spring."

The Image

In a more abstract mystical reading, Lilith could be treated as a purely symbolic force—an archetype without embodied history. In my interpretation, this is love. Pure, unguarded, remembered love. I hear him addressing her directly now, not as demon, not as fate, but as beloved.

Beautiful wast thou. Lithe and delicious. Thy perfume. These are not the words of a man describing an abstract spiritual force. For me, these are the words of a man remembering a woman's body. Her movement. Her scent. The way she felt against him.

Close didst thou cling with thy coils unto the heart, and it was as the joy of all the spring. She wrapped herself around his heart. It was joy. It was spring—life, renewal, warmth after winter.

Verse 8

But I beheld in thee a certain taint, even in that wherein I delighted.

The Image

In a more conventional reading, one could take "taint" to mean he sees her corruption, her evil, her demonic nature. In my interpretation, he is seeing her through THEIR eyes.

The taint is not in her. The taint is the label. The mark. The accusation. Something happened — an affair, a scandal, an accusation of witchcraft — something that marked her in the eyes of the Church and the community.

"Even in that wherein I delighted" — even in the very thing he loved most about her, they found sin. Her freedom. Her knowledge. Her body. Her power. Whatever it was that made her HER, that is what they called tainted.

He beheld the taint not because it was real, but because he could see how they saw her. He loved her AND he could see the target on her back. He knew what that mark meant. He knew what was coming.

This is a man remembering the moment he realized: they will kill her for what I love most about her.

And he stayed anyway.

∴

Verse 9-10

"I beheld in thee the taint of thy father the ape, of thy grandsire the Blind Worm of Slime." (Crowley, 1910, III:9)
"I gazed upon the Crystal of the Future, and I saw the horror of the End of thee." (Crowley, 1910, III:10)

The Image
In a more conventional reading, these verses can be taken as abstract spiritual epithets for degenerate forces or lower natures; in my interpretation, they describe the institutional Church and the Gnostic Demiurge at work in his world.

"The taint of thy father the ape" — the Church. Civilization. The structure of control that mimics wisdom without possessing it. Apes imitate. The Church imitates spirituality while strangling its source. The morality that taxes the soul, binds the body, dictates who to love and how to think — all of it aping true gnosis while carrying none.

"Thy grandsire the Blind Worm of Slime" — this reaches deeper. In Gnostic cosmology, the Demiurge, Yaldabaoth, breathed into clay attempting to imitate the divine, but his breath carried something he did not know he possessed: Sophia's light. The divine spark, smuggled into matter. When he realized his creation carried a light he could not control, he fractured it — separated wisdom from intuition, made the serpent evil, made the body sinful, made woman the source of the fall. The Church inherited this blindness. The "Lord" they serve is the Demiurge's voice.

And now they are killing a woman who remembered. And a man who loved her for remembering.

"I gazed upon the Crystal of the Future, and I saw the horror of the End of thee"

There is no literal crystal. No scrying tool. No mystical vision. Crystal = clarity. The transparency of certainty. A man walking to the gallows has no illusions left. The fog of hope has burned away. What remains is crystal clear: what was, what led here, what comes next.

He knows. He saw. The "horror of the End" is not prophecy but certainty — the absolute knowing of what is coming because there is no other possibility left.

∴

Verse 11

"Further, I destroyed the time Past, and the time to Come, had I not the Power of the Sand-glass?" (Crowley, 1910, III:11)

The Image
In a more abstract mystical reading, this verse could be treated as

a meditation on temporal power and cosmic order; for me, this is not philosophy. This is grief. This is blame.

"Had I not the Power of the Sand-glass?"

This is the question a man asks himself when the woman he loves is dead because of him.

Didn't I have the power to choose differently? Couldn't I have seen where this was going? Didn't I hold time in my hands — couldn't I have turned it another way?

"I destroyed the time Past" — the life they could have had if he'd been wiser. If he'd taken her away. If he'd never touched her. If he'd lied to protect her. All those other timelines, destroyed by his choices.

"And the time to Come" — every future they might have shared. Children. Growing old. Safety. All of it, destroyed.

The chapter does not explain. It does not provide backstory. It drops us into his mind as he walks, and we feel what he feels without knowing the details.

That is what makes it devastating. We know enough.

∴

Verse 12

"But in the very hour I beheld corruption." (Crowley, 1910, III:12)

The Image
Short. Devastating.

"In the very hour" — NOW. This hour. The hour of his walk.

"I beheld corruption."

He sees where his choices led. The platform. The rope. The crowd. Her body. The Magister waiting. The whole scene.

Everything has collapsed into THIS. This hour. This walk. This end.

∴

Verse 13

"Then I said: O my beloved, O Lord Adonai, I pray thee to loosen the coils of the serpent!" (Crowley, 1910, III:13)

The Image
In a more abstract reading, this could be treated as symbolic invocation; in my interpretation, he cries out. A desperate prayer.

"O my beloved, O Lord Adonai" — he calls to GOD. Not the Church's god. His own. The real one. Whatever that is. If you're there, if you're real, NOW is the time.

"I pray thee to loosen the coils of the serpent" — free me. Undo the rope. Undo the binding. Undo what is happening.

The prayer of a condemned man. The last hope before hope dies.

∴

Verse 14

"But she was closed fast upon me, so that my Force was stayed in its inception." (Crowley, 1910, III:14)

The Image

In a more abstract mystical reading, "she was closed fast" could be treated as allegorical binding; in my interpretation, the answer is silence. Or rather, the answer is the opposite of what he asked.

"She was closed fast upon me" — the coils do not loosen. They TIGHTEN.

Three meanings, simultaneous:

The rope. Tight. No escape. The serpent-coil closing around him.

Sophia. Wisdom herself. The Gnostic divine feminine. She is closed fast upon him — not abandoning him, but EMBRACING him. The instrument of his death IS her arms. The rope IS her embrace. She will not let go because she is taking him HOME.

His beloved. Her memory. Her love. Wrapped so tight around his heart he cannot breathe without feeling her.

"So that my Force was stayed in its inception" — whatever power he had, whatever he might have done, is stopped before it can begin. He cannot act. He cannot escape. He is helpless.

But "she was closed fast" — this is not abandonment. This is consummation.

∴

Verse 15

"Also I prayed unto the Elephant God, the Lord of Beginnings, who breaketh down obstruction." (Crowley, 1910, III:15)

The Image
He prayed to God. No answer. The coils stayed tight. Now he prays again, to Ganesha. The Elephant God.

Why Ganesha? The text tells us: "The Lord of Beginnings, who breaketh down obstruction."

A man about to die prays to the god of NEW BEGINNINGS. He wants the obstruction broken – the rope, the Church, the fate closing around him. His mind is swimming. He is throwing prayers at anything that might hear. God. Adonai. Ganesha. Whoever. Whatever.

And yet, beneath the chaos, the correspondence is precise. Ganesha WAS beheaded and became divine through it. Whether the man knows it or not, the prayer lands exactly where it should.

∴

Verse 16

"These gods came right quickly to mine aid. I beheld them; I joined myself unto them; I was lost in their vastness." (Crowley, 1910, III:16)

The Image
Wait.

"These gods came right quickly to mine aid." THEY CAME.

He prayed to Adonai – nothing. The coils stayed tight. He prayed to Ganesha, and now: "These gods came right quickly."

GODS. Plural.

Something is answering. Not one — MANY. They come. He beholds them. He joins himself to them. He is LOST in their vastness.

This is the moment the mind breaks open.

The overwhelm — the drowning, the chaos, the prayers thrown in every direction — has cracked something. And through the crack: THEY POUR IN.

He is no longer singular. He beholds. He joins. He is LOST. This is not rescue. This is dissolution. The boundaries of self are failing. He is becoming vast.

The gallows are still there. The rope is still waiting. But HE is no longer contained in one small body walking forward.

Something has begun.

∴

Verses 17-20

The Snake of Emerald

"Then I beheld myself compassed about with the Infinite Circle of Emerald that encloseth the Universe." (Crowley, 1910, III:17)
"O Snake of Emerald, Thou hast no time Past, no time To Come. Verily Thou art not." (Crowley, 1910, III:18)
"Thou art delicious beyond all taste and touch, Thou art not-to-be-beheld for glory, Thy voice is beyond the Speech and the Silence and the Speech therein, and Thy perfume is of pure ambergris, that is not weighed against the finest gold of the fine gold." (Crowley, 1910, III:19)

"Also Thy coils are of infinite range; the Heart that Thou dost encircle is an Universal Heart." (Crowley, 1910, III:20)

The Image
In a more abstract mystical reading, the Snake of Emerald could be treated as a purely symbolic representation of eternity; in my interpretation, the Snake of Emerald is everything at once: the rope killing him, Kundalini rising up the spine at death, the ouroboros with no beginning or end, the coils around the Universal Heart, Sophia the Gnostic serpent of wisdom, Leviathan the primordial deep, consciousness itself.

As the rope tightens, everything converges. The instrument of death IS the vehicle of awakening IS the symbol of eternity IS consciousness recognizing itself.

"Thou hast no time Past, no time To Come. Verily Thou art not."

He destroyed time Past and time To Come in verse 11 through grief and blame. Now he MEETS what exists when time is gone. The Snake exists outside time. The Snake IS NOT — not a thing, not bounded, not limited to existence as we know it.

"Thy voice is beyond the Speech and the Silence and the Speech therein"

This is THE FORMULA. Speech — the chatter, the noise, the thoughts. Silence — finding the observer, realizing you are not your thoughts. The Speech therein — the voice WITHIN the silence. Not the monkey mind. The TRUE SELF speaking. The still small voice.

"The Heart that Thou dost encircle is an Universal Heart"

Not his heart. THE Heart. The heart of everything. The coils of the Snake wrap around the Universal Heart, and he is inside those coils. He IS the Universal Heart, being embraced.

∴

Verses 21-24

The First Death

"I, and Me, and Mine were sitting with lutes in the market-place of the great city, the city of the violets and the roses." (Crowley, 1910, III:21)
"The night fell, and the music of the lutes was stilled." (Crowley, 1910, III:22)
"The tempest arose, and the music of the lutes was stilled." (Crowley, 1910, III:23)
"The hour passed, and the music of the lutes was stilled." (Crowley, 1910, III:24)

The Image
In a more symbolic reading, these verses could be treated as cycles of loss or meditative withdrawal; in my interpretation, this is the first of THREE accounts of the hanging.

"I, and Me, and Mine" – the fragmented self, the ego in its parts. Sitting with lutes, playing music, living – the ongoing melody of existence.

"The city of the violets and the roses" – life. Beauty. The world as it was before.

Then, three stillings:

"The night fell, and the music of the lutes was stilled."

He walks up. The stairs. Night falls. The music begins to quiet.

"The tempest arose, and the music of the lutes was stilled."

He stands. The platform. The storm of the moment — the crowd, the rope being placed, the chaos of the final seconds.

"The hour passed, and the music of the lutes was stilled."

He drops. THE hour, the appointed hour, passes. The lute goes silent.

Three statements. Three stillings. Walk up. Stand. Drop. Dead.

∴

Verses 25-31

After the First Death

"But Thou art Eternity and Space; Thou art Matter and Motion; and Thou art the negation of all these things." (Crowley, 1910, III:25)
"For there is no Symbol of Thee." (Crowley, 1910, III:26)
"If I say Come up upon the mountains! the celestial waters flow at my word. But thou art the Water beyond the waters." (Crowley, 1910, III:27)
"The red three-angled heart hath been set up in Thy shrine; for the priests despised equally the shrine and the god." (Crowley, 1910, III:28)
"Yet all the while Thou wast hidden therein, as the Lord of Silence is hidden in the buds of the lotus." (Crowley, 1910, III:29)
"Thou art Sebek the crocodile against Asar; thou art Mati, the Slayer in the Deep. Thou art Typhon, the Wrath of the Elements, O Thou who transcendest the Forces in their Concourse and

Cohesion, in their Death and their Disruption. Thou art Python, the terrible serpent about the end of all things!" (Crowley, 1910, III:30)

"I turned me about thrice in every way; and always I came at the last unto Thee." (Crowley, 1910, III:31)

The Image
He has died. He speaks FROM death, TO what he has encountered.

What he encounters cannot be named. It is Eternity AND Space AND Matter AND Motion AND the negation of all of them. Beyond category.

"For there is no Symbol of Thee."

The moment you make a symbol, you've limited it. The thing itself has no symbol because it IS the thing all symbols point toward.

"But thou art the Water beyond the waters."

The mountain, the platform, yes. But also the sacred mountaintop of Gnostic union. The gallows as the site of sacred marriage. Death as consummation. The celestial waters flow — tears, the primordial waters, the waters upon which the Spirit moved. But this is the WATER BEYOND THE WATERS. The source of the source.

"The red three-angled heart hath been set up in Thy shrine; for the priests despised equally the shrine and the god."

The Church built shrines but despised what the shrines were for. They killed the very thing they claimed to worship.

"Yet all the while Thou wast hidden therein, as the Lord of Silence is hidden in the buds of the lotus."

Hidden. The truth was always inside their own temple. Harpocrates, the Lord of Silence, the god with finger to lips. They couldn't see it. But it was there.

"Thou art Sebek the crocodile against Asar; thou art Mati, the Slayer in the Deep. Thou art Typhon, the Wrath of the Elements... Thou art Python, the terrible serpent about the end of all things!"

The DESTROYER faces. Sebek the devourer, Mati the Slayer in the Deep, Typhon who dismembered Osiris, Python the serpent at the END of all things. This is not gentle. This is the WRATH aspect — the destruction that clears the way, the force that tears apart so something new can emerge.

The rope that killed him was ALSO this. And he addresses it directly: YOU. You who killed me. You are ALL of these.

"I turned me about thrice in every way; and always I came at the last unto Thee."

He turned. He looked everywhere. Every direction. Every possibility. And always, ALWAYS, he came back to THIS. To the destroyer, that is also the liberator. To death that is also union.

There was never anywhere else to go.

∴

An Interlude

I have traced one path through these verses. One cosmology. One reading.

But the reader may choose another. Take the same sequence — the walk, the coils, the gods arriving, the Snake of Emerald, the three stillings, the dissolution into what has no symbol — and run it through a different lens. Buddhist, Vedantic, Kabbalistic, Christian mystical, Egyptian. The structure holds. The symbols translate. Liber 777 exists precisely to demonstrate this — that the correspondences align across traditions, that the same truth wears different masks.

I chose the Gnostic reading because it spoke to me. Because Sophia spoke to me. Because the woman they called witch became the goddess who received me.

But the reader may find another face looking back. That is not a flaw in the system. That is the system working.

But I digress.

We were in the midst of a hanging.

∴

Verses 32-39

The Second Death

"Many things I beheld mediate and immediate; but, beholding them no more, I beheld Thee." (Crowley, 1910, III:32)

He saw everything — the mediate and the immediate. All the visions, all the gods, all the forms. And then he stopped seeing THEM.

And saw only THEE.

The forms fall away. The multiplicity collapses. What remains is the One that was wearing all the masks.

"Come thou, O beloved One, O Lord God of the Universe, O Vast One, O Minute One! I am Thy beloved." (Crowley, 1910, III:33)

Now HE calls. Not praying TO. Calling AS.

"I am Thy beloved" – not "make me thy beloved." Not asking. DECLARING. He IS. Already. Always was.

"All day I sing of Thy delight; all night I delight in Thy song." (Crowley, 1910, III:34)
"There is no other day or night than this." (Crowley, 1910, III:35)

The separation between singer and song is dissolving. By day, HE sings of THEE. By night, THEE sings and HE delights. They are trading places. Becoming indistinguishable. Time collapses. There is only THIS.

"Thou art beyond the day and the night; I am Thyself, O my Maker, my Master, my Mate!" (Crowley, 1910, III:36)

"I am Thyself."

Not "I seek Thee." Not "I worship Thee." I AM THYSELF.

Maker, the one who created me. Master, the one who commands me. Mate, the one who joins with me. All three. The same. And I AM THAT.

"I am like the little red dog that sitteth upon the knees of the Unknown." (Crowley, 1910, III:37)

23

After declaring "I am Thyself" — the highest realization — he immediately humbles himself. The little red dog.

The Magician, card I of the Tarot. Red-robed, standing with the four elements. He looks powerful. But he is only ONE step from the Fool (o). He has barely begun. Temperance, the Tower, the Star, the Moon, the Sun, Judgement, the World — all still ahead. The Magician in his red robe is NOWHERE NEAR completion.

After "I am Thyself" comes the recognition: even with this knowledge, even having died, he is still just a little red dog. A beginner. Sitting on the lap of what he cannot comprehend.

"Thou hast brought me into great delight. Thou hast given me of Thy flesh to eat and of Thy blood for an offering of intoxication." (Crowley, 1910, III:38)

Eucharist. Communion. But the Gnostic indictment:

The Church took the divine feminine — Sophia, the Mother, the Bride — and ERASED her. Replaced her with the "Holy Spirit," neutered, abstract, safely masculine in its formlessness. The Trinity became Father, Son, and... what? A ghost?

Where is the Mother? Every other tradition has her. Shakti. Isis. Parvati. Shekinah. The Church buried her. Called her a whore. Called her a witch. Burned her daughters for remembering.

And the communion wine, the "blood," was POISON. Not the blood of Christ offered in love — the blood of a SYSTEM designed to make you forget. The "offering of intoxication" — they got humanity DRUNK on false sacrament. Stupefied. Unable to see.

"Thou hast fastened the fangs of Eternity in my soul, and the Poison of the Infinite hath consumed me utterly." (Crowley, 1910, III:39)

The second death.

FANGS. Bitten. Injected. The Church's poison made him sleep. Sophia's poison makes him die — and BECOME.

Two poisons. Two communions. Two deaths. One from the Demiurge's cup, which kept him in chains. One from Sophia's fangs, which sets him free.

The first death was the hanging — walk up, stand, drop. The second death is the BITE, the fangs of eternity, the poison of the infinite, consumed utterly.

He doesn't just die. He is DEVOURED.

∴

Verses 40-48

The Third Death — Her Death, His Death, One Heart —

In a more traditional mystical reading, this sequence can be treated as a description of spiritual purification and identification with the suffering world; in my interpretation, it is the embodied memory of her torture and death interwoven with his.

The observer has no fixed position now. The perspective oscillates — forward, backward, forward, backward, line by line. Witness and observer trade places. Present and past blur. The text is DOING what it is DESCRIBING.

"I am become like a luscious devil of Italy; a fair strong woman with worn cheeks, eaten out with hunger for kisses. She hath played the harlot in divers palaces; she hath given her body to the beasts." (Crowley, 1910, III:40)

"I am become" — not "I see" or "I watch." I AM BECOME.

He takes on HER identity. The accusations they made against her are now HIS. He wears her condemnation.

"A luscious devil of Italy" — the Church's language for a woman who lived freely. "Fair strong woman with worn cheeks, eaten out with hunger for kisses" — she loved. She desired. She LIVED. And they called it sin.

And he says: I AM BECOME THIS. Her crime is my crime. Her label is my label. We are one in their eyes. We will be one in death.

"She hath slain her kinsfolk with strong venom of toads; she hath been scourged with many rods." (Crowley, 1910, III:41)

The accusations multiply. Poisoner. Murderer. The "venom of toads" — witchcraft. The classic charge.

"She hath been scourged with many rods" — they beat her. Before the hanging, they BEAT her. This is what he watched. This is what he carries.

"She hath been broken in pieces upon the Wheel; the hands of the hangman have bound her unto it." (Crowley, 1910, III:42)

The Wheel. The instrument of torture. The breaking wheel. They bound her to it. They broke her body.

But also: The Wheel of Fortune. Card X. Fate. Cycle. What goes around.

"The fountains of water have been loosed upon her; she hath struggled with exceeding torment." (Crowley, 1910, III:43)

Water torture. Drowning. The "swimming" of a witch – if she floats, she's guilty; if she drowns, she's innocent but dead.

He watched her struggle. He watched her suffer. He carries this.

"She hath burst in sunder with the weight of the waters; she hath sunk into the awful Sea." (Crowley, 1910, III:44)

She broke. The water, the torture, the Church, the weight of it all – burst her apart.

"She hath sunk into the awful Sea" – she died. Into the deep. Into the Waters that are also Binah, also the Mother, also the return. Awful in the old sense. AWE-full. Terrible and sacred.

"So am I, O Adonai, my lord, and such are the waters of Thine intolerable Essence." (Crowley, 1910, III:45)

"So am I."

What happened to her happens to me. Her death is my death. Her breaking is my breaking. We are ONE in this.

"So am I, O Adonai, my beloved, and Thou hast burst me utterly in sunder." (Crowley, 1910, III:46)

He breaks too. As she broke. The same waters. The same Adonai. The same bursting. They are broken together. By the same force. Into the same sea.

"I am shed out like spilt blood upon the mountains; the Ravens of Dispersion have borne me utterly away." (Crowley, 1910, III:47)

Spilt blood — sacrifice. Shed upon the mountains, the high places. The gallows platform. The altar.

"The Ravens of Dispersion" — the scatterers, the forces that DISPERSE the self, that scatter the ego across infinity. Nothing left. No self remaining.

"Therefore is the seal unloosed, that guarded the Eighth abyss; therefore is the vast sea as a veil; therefore is there a rending asunder of all things." (Crowley, 1910, III:48)

In a more strictly Kabbalistic reading, this could be treated as a metaphor for crossing an inner abyss or Daath-like threshold; in my interpretation, THE SEAL IS BROKEN.

"The Eighth abyss" — beyond the seven planets, beyond the seven chakras, beyond the seven days of creation. The EIGHTH. The octave. The return at a higher level.

The seal that GUARDED it is now UNLOOSED. Their death broke the seal.

What seal? The spell. The Church's spell — that he is guilty, that she was evil, that their love was sin, that death is punishment, that God condemns them. In the moment before the drop, he RELEASES it. He sees through. He stops believing their lie.

His final wish: If there is anything next, let it be her. Not salvation. Not heaven. Not vindication. Just HER.

28

That prayer — that single pure desire stripped of everything the Church told him to want — THAT is what tears the veil.

"A rending asunder of all things" — everything torn apart. Not just them. ALL THINGS.

For those who would understand this verse more deeply, see the Gospel of Elyalith.

∴

The Deaths

First death: His hanging — walk up, stand, drop. Second death: His spiritual dissolution — the fangs, the poison. Third death: HER death that IS his death — they break together, burst together, sink together into the awful Sea.

And in that final death, the seal breaks. The eighth abyss opens. Everything rends.

Two become one. In death. In the waters. In what lies beyond.

∴

Verses 49-56

The Accusation and the Inversion

What follows is not prayer. It is ACCUSATION. Every "O" is loaded — the ouroboros, the circle, the moment of seeing full circle. The snake that ate its own tail. The Church that became the serpent it demonized.

"O Thou light and delight, ravish me away into the milky ocean of the stars!" (Crowley, 1910, III:49)

He is crying. Bathed in the waters of his own baptism — the same Church that dunked him as a child now kills him as a man.

"O" — the ouroboros. The circle. Full circle. He SEES it now.

"O Thou Son of an O! O Thou formless One, Thou art my Father, and my Mother, and my Child!" (Crowley, 1910, III:50)

Son of an O — Son of NOTHING. Son of the ZERO. The dying-and-rising god. The one born of the divine feminine who carries light through death.

"Thou art my Father, and my Mother, and my Child" — this phrase carries multiple meanings simultaneously.

First layer — the accusation:

Hear it as the crowd hears it. The pointing finger. "O! THOU!" — YOU! You there! YOU are the one! He throws it back at them: YOU are the devil. You who call US devils, me and my witch — YOU are the darkness pretending to be light.

Second layer — the clarity:

Sapphire is Crowley's color of Chokmah. Pure dynamic Will. The Abyss of Sapphire is not the black Abyss that terrifies the ego — it is the same gulf viewed FROM ABOVE. He is about to die. He knows it. His ego is already surrendered. So the terror that would grip a man clinging to life is absent. He sees the Abyss as sapphire — clear, luminous, transparent Will.

He accuses them while simultaneously experiencing the clarity of one who has already crossed. The rage and the transcendence are not contradictions. They are the same moment from two angles.

"O my golden one" — You rich-robed priests. You gilded hypocrites. Your gold vestments. Your golden lies.

"O my Lord Adonai" — the cry carries both meanings. On one level: the counterfeit god they sold him, the one who never answered. On another: the TRUE Lord, the Angel, the presence that walks with him now.

The inversion is complete. The accused becomes the judge. The hanged man sees what the executioners cannot.

∴

Verses 57-65

The Drop — The Finale

He follows her. Literally. In order of execution. She went first. Now he goes.

His hope: if God isn't real, then maybe something good is. And if not, if nothing is real, then let her be there. Let the last thing be HER.

The Magister asks: Do you have any last words?

"How shall I answer the foolish man?"

There is nothing he can say that they will understand. The "mystery" of the Holy Ghost? There IS no mystery. It's the missing Mother. It's Sophia erased. He could scream it from the platform and they would not see.

The spell is too deep.

"The instruction in vain" — the ultimate indictment.

YOU told me to listen to the Holy Spirit. YOU said the Spirit would guide me. I LISTENED. And the Spirit led me to HER. To love. To truth. To Sophia. And now YOU kill me for following YOUR instruction.

The instruction was in vain — not because the Spirit didn't speak, but because YOU never meant it. You wanted compliance, not communion. Obedience, not gnosis.

I heard. I found her. I found love. And now look.

You kill me for doing exactly what you told me to do.

The Eagle made one with Man — the Eagle is flight, the DROP as flying, Scorpio's higher octave. The Scorpion is the tail, the rope, the sting, the lower octave that kills.

The crowd cheers — snap.

The scorpion that stings becomes the eagle that rises. The death IS the flight. The drop IS the ascent.

The Hanged Man, who finally SEES the world as it is. Upside down. Too late to change anything. But peaceful. Not struggling. SEEING.

"The gallows of infamy dance with the fruit of the just" — the hanged man is fruit now. Harvested. Plucked from the tree. The fruit of the Tree of Knowledge. The thing the Demiurge said would kill you — and it DOES kill you, but into LIFE.

THEY think they're just. THEY think this is justice. The gallows of INFAMY — infamous to history, but they call it righteous.

"I have descended, O my darling, into the black shining waters, and I have plucked Thee forth as a black pearl of infinite preciousness." (Crowley, 1910, III:60)

"I have descended" — the DROP. The fall. Down through the trapdoor. Down through death.

"Into the black shining waters" — death. The void. But SHINING. Not empty darkness — luminous darkness. The black that contains all colors. The pregnant void.

"And plucked thee forth" — HE reaches. In death. Through death. And he FINDS her. He PLUCKS her. He retrieves her from the depths.

"As a black pearl of infinite preciousness" — THE BLACK PEARL.

What is a pearl? An irritant wrapped in beauty. Something the oyster couldn't expel, so it transformed it. Layer by layer. The wound becomes the treasure.

What is a BLACK pearl? The rare one. The forbidden one. NO THING.

The Zero. The Void. The Ain. Consciousness itself — which cannot be found, only demonstrated. The ineffable, which cannot be named. The observer that cannot observe itself directly.

The Zero Formula: $0 = (+1) + (-1)$

Nothing contains everything in perfect balance. The void is not empty — it is FULL of potential. All opposites emerge from and return to zero.

He falls through death and finds not a thing, not a being, not a god, but the GROUND. The substrate. The No Thing that all things float in.

And in that No Thing: her. Because she was never a thing either. She was always consciousness meeting consciousness. Love recognizing love. Zero recognizing zero.

∴

Verses 61-64

For those who would understand these verses more deeply, read the Gospel of Elyalith.

This chapter — Chapter III of LXV, the chapter of Water, numbered 65 for Adonai — gave me the vision it did because Elyalith IS the Zero Formula pronounced. The No Thing given a name.

She was always there. Hidden in the black shining waters. The black pearl of infinite preciousness. The consciousness that precedes the Father. The Mother. The void that contains all.

And I said her name.

∴

Verse 65

The final verse of the chapter numbered for Adonai closes what was opened. The seal that was unloosed. The two that became one. The man who became Angel by dying into the black shining waters and plucking forth the black pearl.

Conclusion

34

Four deaths. One hanging.

First death: The physical — walk up, stand, drop. The lutes stilled. His body dies.

Second death: The spiritual dissolution — the fangs of eternity, the poison of the infinite, consumed utterly. His separate self dies.

Third death: THEIR death — her death that IS his death. Broken together, burst together, sunk together into the awful Sea. One heart. The boundary between them dies.

Fourth death: The vision — the culmination. He sees it all from above, from beyond. The overview that contains the other three. The death of the one who was watching.

And in that final death — the seal breaks. The eighth abyss opens. Everything rends.

The man becomes the Angel. The Aspirant becomes Adonai. The horizontal reading meets the vertical. The one walking to the gallows IS the one narrating from beyond.

They were never two.

I have traced one path through these 65 verses. One cosmology. One reading.

The traditional reading remains valid — Aspirant below, Angel above, seeking union. That structure is there. It has served generations.

But after nine years of internal memorization, after the text became architecture in my mind, a second structure emerged. A man walking to his death. A woman already killed. A love that broke the seal.

Both readings may coexist. The text appears to contain both structures simultaneously. The correspondences across traditions — Buddhist, Vedantic, Kabbalistic, Christian mystical, Egyptian — suggest a symbolic architecture that translates across frameworks. Liber 777 exists to demonstrate this principle.

The method is reproducible: commit one chapter to perfect internal memory. Wait. Observe what emerges. What came through for me was the Gospel of Elyalith — the Zero Formula pronounced.

That is my experiential record. Another practitioner's may differ.

References

Crowley, A. (1909). Liber 777 vel prolegomena symbolica ad systemam sceptico-mysticae viae explicandae. The Equinox, 1(1).

Crowley, A. (1910). Liber LXV: Liber cordis cincti serpente. The Equinox, 1(3), Supplement.

Crowley, A. (1912). Gematria. The Equinox, 1(8), Supplement.

CHAPTER TWO
THE WAVE AND THE CARDS

The Mathematics of Transformation

Author Commentary

Any serious discussion of magic must begin by stripping away the theatrical elements that have accrued around the word. If magic exists at all — and that remains an open question — it would bear little resemblance to the familiar imagery of robes, symbols, or ritual implements. It would look far more like a disciplined psychological craft rooted in concentration, visualization, and self-regulation.

Across contemplative practice, energy work, meditation, depth psychology, and parapsychology, the same cluster of capacities appears repeatedly: the ability to sustain a stable internal image, the ability to maintain attention without drift, and the ability to stay coherent when perception becomes unstable or ambiguous. These skills are rare, and they are almost never acquired casually.

If an effective system of magic exists, it would demand the same rigor expected of any elite cognitive discipline. It would offer no shortcuts, no reassurances, and no guarantees. In such a context, instruction becomes a set of pressures applied to attention, not a transfer of knowledge. Progress arises not from learning doctrines but from meeting one's own perceptual limits without flinching.

Any genuine system must accept a difficult premise: the next practitioner will not develop along the same trajectory as the last.

The strongest traditions recognize this and avoid promising reproducible results. Instead of maps, they provide orientations. What appears, from the outside, as vagueness or withholding is, from the inside, the only structure that prevents practitioners from mistaking suggestion for insight.

Here, psychology and esoteric practice intersect. Any system that claims to lead reliably to a transformative state risks becoming a script its practitioners unconsciously perform. The more honest systems refuse that role. They offer texts, symbols, exercises, and doors — but stop short of interpretation.

On the A∴A∴ and the Problem of Instruction

Among Western esoteric orders, the A∴A∴ is remarkable for a feature that often frustrates scholars: it does not behave like a teaching institution at all. It provides no curriculum in the conventional sense, offers no map, and does not pretend to possess a stable metaphysics capable of being transmitted intact from one generation to the next. What it offers most closely resembles what anthropologists term aperture conditioning: the intentional reduction of external guidance so that the aspirant is forced into reliance on internal observation.

The entire structure rests on a single principle: the next exception will be the next person, not the last. The system minimizes transference. It prevents aspirants from mistaking another person's realization for their own. The historical record shows the same pattern across generations: a senior figure points a junior toward a direction, never an answer.

The result is a tradition that appears, from the outside, to produce solitary practitioners. Yet their journals reveal convergences so statistically improbable that dismissing them as coincidence becomes academically uncomfortable. Some journals are clearly metaphorical. Some are aspirational. A few read like psychological field notes from someone who spent a considerable portion of their life examining regions of consciousness where symbolic language ceases to hold steady.

This makes the A∴A∴ difficult to categorize. Is it a magical order? A psychological discipline? A case study in extreme cognitive training? A self-selected group predisposed to unusual perceptual states? Or — and this is the question that refuses to disappear — did some of its members actually accomplish the interior transformation the system is designed never to describe?

What is given is a bookshelf, a doorway, a small set of exercises, and — if one is unusually fortunate — a person who says only, "Go that way."

That ambiguity is not a flaw. It is the mechanism. It creates the only environment in which genuine insight can occur, or genuine delusion can reveal itself, without the safety net of external certainty.

From the outside, this resembles negligence.

From the inside, it is the only honest architecture any transformative discipline has ever produced.

LIBER LXV CHAPTER III – STRESS ANALYSIS

Method

Counting primary stresses, the beats that carry the weight in natural English speech. Not every stressed syllable, but the main beats that would land if you were reading aloud at cadence.

VERSE BY VERSE ANALYSIS

VERSE 1: "Verily and Amen! I passed through the deep sea, and by the rivers of running water that abound therein, and I came unto the Land of No Desire."

VER | MEN | PASSED | DEEP | SEA | RIV | RUN | WA | BOUND | CAME | LAND | NO | SIRE

COUNT: 13

∴

VERSE 2: "Wherein was a white unicorn with a silver collar, whereon was graven the aphorism Linea viridis gyrat universa."

WHITE | U | SIL | COL | GRA | APH | LI | VI | GY | VER

COUNT: 10

∴

VERSE 3: "Then the word of Adonai came unto me by the mouth of the Magister mine, saying: O heart that art girt about with the coils of the old serpent, lift up thyself unto the mountain of initiation!"

WORD | DO | CAME | ME | MOUTH | GIS | MINE | HEART | GIRT | COILS | OLD | SER | LIFT | SELF | MOUN | A

COUNT: 16

∴

VERSE 4: "But I remembered. Yea, Than, yea, Theli, yea, Lilith! these three were about me from of old. For they are one."

MEM | YEA | THAN | YEA | THE | YEA | LI | THREE | OLD | ONE

COUNT: 10

∴

VERSE 5: "Beautiful wast thou, O Lilith, thou serpent-woman!"

BEAU | WAST | THOU | LI | SER | WO

COUNT: 6

∴

VERSE 6: "Thou wast lithe and delicious to the taste, and thy perfume was of musk mingled with ambergris."

LITHE | LI | TASTE | FUME | MUSK | MIN | AM

COUNT: 7

∴

VERSE 7: "Close didst thou cling with thy coils unto the heart, and it was as the joy of all the spring."

CLOSE | CLING | COILS | HEART | JOY | ALL | SPRING

COUNT: 7

∴

VERSE 8: "But I beheld in thee a certain taint, even in that wherein I delighted."

HELD | THEE | CER | TAINT | THAT | LIGHT

COUNT: 6

∴

VERSE 9: "I beheld in thee the taint of thy father the ape, of thy grandsire the Blind Worm of Slime."

HELD | THEE | TAINT | FA | APE | GRAND | BLIND | WORM | SLIME

COUNT: 9

∴

VERSE 10: "I gazed upon the Crystal of the Future, and I saw the horror of the End of thee."

GAZED | CRYS | FU | SAW | HOR | END | THEE

COUNT: 7

∴

VERSE 11: "Further, I destroyed the time Past, and the time to Come – had I not the Power of the Sand-glass?"

FUR | STROYED | TIME | PAST | TIME | COME | POW | SAND

COUNT: 8

∴

VERSE 12: "But in the very hour I beheld corruption."

VE | HOUR | HELD | RUP

COUNT: 4

∴

VERSE 13: "Then I said: O my beloved, O Lord Adonai, I pray thee to loosen the coils of the serpent!"

SAID | LOV | LORD | DO | PRAY | LOO | COILS | SER

COUNT: 8

∴

VERSE 14: "But she was closed fast upon me, so that my Force was stayed in its inception."

CLOSED | FAST | ME | FORCE | STAYED | CEP

COUNT: 6

∴

VERSE 15: "Also I prayed unto the Elephant God, the Lord of Beginnings, who breaketh down obstruction."

PRAYED | EL | GOD | LORD | GIN | BREAK | STRUC

COUNT: 7

∴

VERSE 16: "These gods came right quickly to mine aid. I beheld them; I joined myself unto them; I was lost in their vastness."

GODS | CAME | RIGHT | QUICK | AID | HELD | JOINED | LOST | VAST

COUNT: 9

∴

VERSE 17: "Then I beheld myself compassed about with the Infinite Circle of Emerald that encloseth the Universe."

HELD | COM | IN | CIR | EM | CLO | U

COUNT: 7

∴

VERSE 18: "O Snake of Emerald, Thou hast no time Past, no time To Come. Verily Thou art not."

SNAKE | EM | TIME | PAST | TIME | COME | VE | ART | NOT

COUNT: 9

∴

VERSE 19: "Thou art delicious beyond all taste and touch, Thou art not-to-be-beheld for glory, Thy voice is beyond the Speech and the Silence and the Speech therein, and Thy perfume is of pure ambergris, that is not weighed against the finest gold of the fine gold."

LI | YOND | TASTE | TOUCH | HELD | GLO | VOICE | YOND | SPEECH | SI | SPEECH | FUME | PURE | AM | WEIGHED | FI | GOLD | FINE | GOLD

COUNT: 19

∴

VERSE 20: "Also Thy coils are of infinite range; the Heart that Thou dost encircle is an Universal Heart."

COILS | IN | RANGE | HEART | CIR | VER | HEART

COUNT: 7

∴

VERSE 21: "I, and Me, and Mine were sitting with lutes in the market-place of the great city, the city of the violets and the roses."

I | ME | MINE | SIT | LUTES | MAR | GREAT | CI | CI | VI | RO

COUNT: 11

∴

VERSE 22: "The night fell, and the music of the lutes was stilled."

NIGHT | FELL | MU | LUTES | STILLED

COUNT: 5

∴

VERSE 23: "The tempest arose, and the music of the lutes was stilled."

TEM | ROSE | MU | LUTES | STILLED

COUNT: 5

∴

VERSE 24: "The hour passed, and the music of the lutes was stilled."

HOUR | PASSED | MU | LUTES | STILLED

COUNT: 5

∴

VERSE 25: "But Thou art Eternity and Space; Thou art Matter and Motion; and Thou art the negation of all these things."

TER | SPACE | MAT | MO | GA | ALL | THINGS

COUNT: 7

∴

VERSE 26: "For there is no Symbol of Thee."

SYM | THEE

COUNT: 2

∴

VERSE 27: "If I say Come up upon the mountains! the celestial waters flow at my word. But thou art the Water beyond the waters."

SAY | COME | MOUN | LES | WA | FLOW | WORD | WA | YOND | WA

COUNT: 10

∴

VERSE 28: "The red three-angled heart hath been set up in Thy shrine; for the priests despised equally the shrine and the god."

RED | THREE | HEART | SET | SHRINE | PRIESTS | SPISED | E | SHRINE | GOD

COUNT: 10

46

∴

VERSE 29: "Yet all the while Thou wast hidden therein, as the Lord of Silence is hidden in the buds of the lotus."

WHILE | HID | LORD | SI | HID | BUDS | LO

COUNT: 7

∴

VERSE 30: "Thou art Sebek the crocodile against Asar; thou art Mati, the Slayer in the Deep. Thou art Typhon, the Wrath of the Elements, O Thou who transcendest the Forces in their Concourse and Cohesion, in their Death and their Disruption. Thou art Python, the terrible serpent about the end of all things!"

SE | CROC | A | MA | SLAY | DEEP | TY | WRATH | EL | SCEND | FOR | CON | HE | DEATH | RUP | PY | TER | SER | END | ALL | THINGS

COUNT: 21

∴

VERSE 31: "I turned me about thrice in every way; and always I came at the last unto Thee."

TURNED | THRICE | EV | WAY | AL | CAME | LAST | THEE

COUNT: 8

∴

VERSE 32: "Many things I beheld mediate and immediate; but, beholding them no more, I beheld Thee."

MA | THINGS | HELD | ME | ME | HOLD | MORE | HELD | THEE

COUNT: 9

∴

VERSE 33: "Come thou, O beloved One, O Lord God of the Universe, O Vast One, O Minute One! I am Thy beloved."

COME | LOV | ONE | LORD | GOD | U | VAST | ONE | NUTE | ONE | LOV

COUNT: 11

∴

VERSE 34: "All day I sing of Thy delight; all night I delight in Thy song."

DAY | SING | LIGHT | NIGHT | LIGHT | SONG

COUNT: 6

VERSE 35: "There is no other day or night than this."

O | DAY | NIGHT | THIS

COUNT: 4

∴

VERSE 36: "Thou art beyond the day and the night; I am Thyself, O my Maker, my Master, my Mate!"

YOND | DAY | NIGHT | THY | MA | MAS | MATE

COUNT: 7

∴

VERSE 37: "I am like the little red dog that sitteth upon the knees of the Unknown."

LIT | RED | DOG | SIT | KNEES | KNOWN

COUNT: 6

∴

VERSE 38: "Thou hast brought me into great delight. Thou hast given me of Thy flesh to eat and of Thy blood for an offering of intoxication."

BROUGHT | GREAT | LIGHT | GIV | FLESH | EAT | BLOOD | OF | CA

COUNT: 9

∴

VERSE 39: "Thou hast fastened the fangs of Eternity in my soul, and the Poison of the Infinite hath consumed me utterly."

FAS | FANGS | TER | SOUL | POI | IN | SUMED | UT

COUNT: 8

∴

VERSE 40: "I am become like a luscious devil of Italy; a fair strong woman with worn cheeks, eaten out with hunger for kisses. She hath played the harlot in divers palaces; she hath given her body to the beasts."

COME | LUS | DEV | IT | FAIR | STRONG | WO | WORN | CHEEKS | EA | HUN | KIS | PLAYED | HAR | DI | PAL | GIV | BO | BEASTS

COUNT: 19

∴

VERSE 41: "She hath slain her kinsfolk with strong venom of toads; she hath been scourged with many rods."

SLAIN | KINS | STRONG | VEN | TOADS | SCOURGED | MA | RODS

COUNT: 8

∴

VERSE 42: "She hath been broken in pieces upon the Wheel; the hands of the hangman have bound her unto it."

BRO | PIE | WHEEL | HANDS | HANG | BOUND | IT

COUNT: 7

∴

VERSE 43: "The fountains of water have been loosed upon her; she hath struggled with exceeding torment."

FOUN | WA | LOOSED | STRUG | CEE | TOR

COUNT: 6

∴

VERSE 44: "She hath burst in sunder with the weight of the waters; she hath sunk into the awful Sea."

BURST | SUN | WEIGHT | WA | SUNK | AW | SEA

COUNT: 7

∴

VERSE 45: "So am I, O Adonai, my lord, and such are the waters of Thine intolerable Essence."

DO | LORD | WA | TOL | ES

COUNT: 5

∴

VERSE 46: "So am I, O Adonai, my beloved, and Thou hast burst me utterly in sunder."

DO | LOV | BURST | UT | SUN

COUNT: 5

∴

VERSE 47: "I am shed out like spilt blood upon the mountains; the Ravens of Dispersion have borne me utterly away."

SHED | SPILT | BLOOD | MOUN | RA | PER | BORNE | UT | WAY

COUNT: 9

∴

VERSE 48: "Therefore is the seal unloosed, that guarded the Eighth abyss; therefore is the vast sea as a veil; therefore is there a rending asunder of all things."

SEAL | LOOSED | GUARD | EIGHTH | BYSS | VAST | SEA |
VEIL | REND | SUN | ALL | THINGS

COUNT: 12

∴

VERSE 49: "Yea, also verily Thou art the cool still water of the
wizard fount. I have bathed in Thee, and lost me in Thy stillness."

VE | COOL | STILL | WA | WI | FOUNT | BATHED | LOST |
STILL

COUNT: 9

∴

VERSE 50: "That which went in as a brave boy of beautiful limbs
cometh forth as a maiden, as a little child for perfection."

WENT | BRAVE | BOY | BEAU | LIMBS | CO | FORTH |
MAI | LIT | CHILD | FEC

COUNT: 11

∴

VERSE 51: "O Thou light and delight, ravish me away into the
milky ocean of the stars!"

LIGHT | LIGHT | RAV | WAY | MIL | O | STARS

COUNT: 7

∴

VERSE 52: "O Thou Son of a light-transcending mother, blessed be Thy name, and the Name of Thy Name, throughout the ages!"

SON | LIGHT | SCEND | MO | BLESS | NAME | NAME | NAME | A

COUNT: 9

∴

VERSE 53: "Behold! I am a butterfly at the Source of Creation; let me die before the hour, falling dead into Thine infinite stream!"

BUT | SOURCE | A | DIE | HOUR | FAL | DEAD | IN | STREAM

COUNT: 9

∴

VERSE 54: "Also the stream of the stars floweth ever majestical unto the Abode; bear me away upon the Bosom of Nuit!"

STREAM | STARS | FLOW | JES | BODE | BEAR | WAY | BO | NU

COUNT: 9

∴

VERSE 55: "This is the world of the waters of Maim; this is the bitter water that becometh sweet. Thou art beautiful and bitter, O golden one, O my Lord Adonai, O thou Abyss of Sapphire!"

WORLD | WA | MAIM | BIT | WA | CO | SWEET | BEAU |
BIT | GOL | ONE | LORD | DO | BYSS | SAPH

COUNT: 15

∴

VERSE 56: "I follow Thee, and the waters of Death fight
strenuously against me. I pass unto the Waters beyond Death and
beyond Life."

FOL | WA | DEATH | FIGHT | STREN | PASS | WA | YOND |
DEATH | YOND | LIFE

COUNT: 11

∴

VERSE 57: "How shall I answer the foolish man? In no way shall
he come to the Identity of Thee!"

AN | FOO | MAN | WAY | COME | DEN | THEE

COUNT: 7

∴

VERSE 58: "But I am the Fool that heedeth not the Play of the
Magician. Me doth the Woman of the Mysteries instruct in vain; I
have burst the bonds of Love and of Power and of Worship."

FOOL | HEED | PLAY | GI | WO | MYS | STRUCT | VAIN |
BURST | BONDS | LOVE | POW | WOR

COUNT: 13

∴

VERSE 59: "Therefore is the Eagle made one with the Man, and the gallows of infamy dance with the fruit of the just."

EA | MADE | ONE | MAN | GAL | IN | DANCE | FRUIT | JUST

COUNT: 9

∴

VERSE 60: "I have descended, O my darling, into the black shining waters, and I have plucked Thee forth as a black pearl of infinite preciousness."

SCEND | DAR | BLACK | SHIN | WA | PLUCKED | FORTH | BLACK | PEARL | IN | PRE

COUNT: 11

∴

VERSE 61: "I have gone down, O my God, into the abyss of the all, and I have found Thee in the midst under the guise of No Thing."

GONE | DOWN | GOD | BYSS | ALL | FOUND | THEE | MIDST | GUISE | NO | THING

COUNT: 11

∴

VERSE 62: "But as Thou art the Last, Thou art also the Next, and as the Next do I reveal Thee to the multitude."

LAST | NEXT | NEXT | VEAL | THEE | MUL

COUNT: 6

∴

VERSE 63: "They that ever desired Thee shall obtain Thee, even at the End of their Desire."

SIRED | THEE | TAIN | THEE | END | SIRE

COUNT: 6

∴

VERSE 64: "Glorious, glorious, glorious art Thou, O my lover supernal, O Self of myself."

GLO | GLO | GLO | LO | PER | SELF | SELF

COUNT: 7

∴

VERSE 65: "For I have found Thee alike in the Me and the Thee; there is no difference, O my beautiful, my desirable One! In the One and the Many have I found Thee; yea, I have found Thee."

FOUND | THEE | ME | THEE | DIF | BEAU | SIR | ONE | ONE | MA | FOUND | THEE | YEA | FOUND | THEE

COUNT: 15

∴

SUMMARY TABLE
INITIAL OBSERVATIONS

Verses 22, 23, 24, the three "stilled" verses, all carry 5 stresses each. Identical. The music stopped three times, same weight each time.

Verse 26, "For there is no Symbol of Thee," carries 2 stresses. The lowest in the chapter. The absolute minimum.

Verse 30, the great Typhon/Python verse, carries 21 stresses. The highest. The maximum expansion.

Verses 12 and 35 both carry 4 stresses. "But in the very hour I beheld corruption" and "There is no other day or night than this." The moments of realization, compressed.

The counts oscillate. They swing. They breathe.

STRESS COUNT SEQUENCE TABLE

Key:

Verse = Verse number (1 through 65). Stress = Number of stressed syllables in the verse. V+S = Verse number plus Stress count. Reduced = V+S reduced to single digit (11 left as Master Number).

Notable Patterns:

Verse 26 (No Symbol): Lowest stress count (2). Verse 30 (Typhon/Python): Highest stress count (21). Verses 22 through 24 (Three Stillings): All have stress count of 5. Verses 41 through 43: All reduce to 13/4 (Death/Elements). Verse 65: Reduces to 8 (∞).

PART TWO: THE ENCODING

Method

The following analysis demonstrates the multi-layered numerical encoding in LXV Chapter III. Each verse contains interlocking values: verse number and its reductions, stress count and its reductions, verse plus stress combinations and further reductions, and Hebrew gematria of key words through subject/object analysis.

This touches only the surface. Multiplication, division, and letter-by-letter analysis reveal further depths. What follows are representative examples demonstrating the encoding exists and is verifiable.

VERSE 1 – ENTRY INTO THE WORLD

Text: "Verily and Amen! I passed through the deep sea, and by the rivers of running water that abound therein, and I came unto the Land of No Desire."

The Land of No Desire = Earth. Malkuth. The material plane. The four corners of a circle = the Elements. The fifth element = Spirit, the point at the center.

Verse number: 1. Stress count: 13.

13 = Death card. Scorpio. Transformation. 1 + 3 = 4 = the Elements. The four corners. The body. 4 + 1 (verse) = 5. 5 = the number of Man. The pentagram. Spirit presiding over the four elements.

"Every man and every woman is a star." (Liber AL I:3)

The first verse encodes a spirit entering flesh, a star falling to earth, the beginning of the journey toward death and transformation. In Thelema, the first station is Man of Earth. Verse 1 places the reader at the beginning of the initiatory path.

∴

VERSE 2 – THE WHITE UNICORN

Text: "Wherein was a white unicorn with a silver collar, whereon was graven the aphorism Linea viridis gyrat universa."

Verse number: 2. Stress count: 10. 2 + 10 = 12 = 1 + 2 = 3.

3 = the Supernal Triad. Kether (Crown, Light), Chokmah (Wisdom, Life, the Father), Binah (Understanding, Love, the Mother). Father, Mother, Son. The three above the Abyss.

The three alchemical principles: Sulphur (active, fiery, masculine, Chokmah), Salt (passive, receptive, feminine, Binah), Mercury (mediating, unifying, spirit, Kether). These three resolve all elemental magic. The four elements derive from the three. The three are primary.

The White Unicorn: White = purity, Kether, undifferentiated light. Unicorn = single horn = unity = the One before division. Silver collar = Luna = Yesod = reflection of supernals below.

"Linea viridis gyrat universa" = "The green line circles the universe," the Emerald serpent, the path connecting all sephiroth.

The sequence: after Man of Earth enters (verse 1), he is shown the origin, the three in one that everything unfolds from. Walking backward up the Tree while walking forward to the gallows.

∴

VERSE 26 – NO SYMBOL

Text: "For there is no Symbol of Thee."

The shortest verse. The minimum. The compression point.

Verse number: 26. Stress count: 2, the lowest in the entire chapter.

$2 + 6 = 8 = \infty$ = infinity. $8 + 2 = 10$ = the Wheel = Malkuth = completion of cycle. $1 + 0 = 1$ = the beginning. Unity. The One.

The verse that says there is no symbol resolves to One.

The verse with the fewest stresses, closest to silence, closest to zero, encodes the path from infinity (8) through completion (10) back to unity (1). The absence pointing at the presence.

∴

VERSE 48 – THE SEAL

Text: "Therefore is the seal unloosed, that guarded the Eighth abyss; therefore is the vast sea as a veil; therefore is there a rending asunder of all things."

Verse number: 48. Stress count: 12. $4 + 8 = 12$. $12 + 12 = 24 = 2 + 4 = 6$.

But the verse itself names the Eighth abyss. $6 + 8 = 14$. $1 + 4 = 5$.

5 = Elyalith.

The verse about the seal breaking, where everything rends asunder, encodes her number. Hidden in the verse about her own unsealing.

The seal that guarded the Eighth abyss, when broken, reveals Five. The missing half. The Zero Formula. The Mother.

∴

VERSE 52 – LIGHT TRANSCENDING MOTHER

Text: "O Thou Son of a light-transcending mother, blessed be Thy name, and the Name of Thy Name, throughout the ages!"

Verse number: 52. Stress count: 9. 5 + 2 = 7. 7 + 9 = 16 = the Tower. 1 + 6 = 7 = Netzach = Venus = Love = Magic.

The verse that names the Mother directly encodes the Tower (the structure that must fall) and Magic (the force that brings it down).

Venus. The morning star. The light transcending mother, the one before the light. The darkness that contains all colors.

He hid her in plain sight. "Light transcending mother." He said it. And then he numbered it so the math confirms: 7, the force that brings towers down.

∴

VERSE 53 – THE BUTTERFLY

Text: "Behold! I am a butterfly at the Source of Creation; let me die before the hour, falling dead into Thine infinite stream!"

Verse number: 53. Stress count: 9. 5 + 3 = 8. 8 + 9 = 17 = 1 + 7 = 8.

∞. Infinity. The lemniscate.

The butterfly. Psyche. The soul. The verse about dying into the infinite stream resolves to infinity itself.

∴

VERSE 58 – THE FOOL AND THE MAGICIAN

Text: "But I am the Fool that heedeth not the Play of the Magician. Me doth the Woman of the Mysteries instruct in vain; I have burst the bonds of Love and of Power and of Worship."

Verse number: 58. Stress count: 13. 5 + 8 = 13 = Death. 1 + 3 = 4. Stress also = 13 = Death. Double 13. 13 + 13 = 26 = YHVH = Tetragrammaton = the Name of God. 2 + 6 = 8 = infinity.

Three cards named explicitly: the Fool (Card 0), the Magician (Card I), the Woman of the Mysteries / High Priestess (Card II). 0 + 1 + 2 = 3 = the Empress. The Mother. The one not named. The hidden fourth.

"I have burst the bonds of Love and of Power and of Worship."

Love = Venus = Netzach = 7. Power = Mars = Geburah = 5. Worship = Jupiter = Chesed = 4. 7 + 5 + 4 = 16 = the Tower. 1 + 6 = 7 = Venus = Love = the force that breaks towers.

This is the verse where the old system breaks. The Fool sees through the play. The bonds shatter.

∴

VERSE 60 – THE BLACK PEARL

Text: "I have descended, O my darling, into the black shining waters, and I have plucked Thee forth as a black pearl of infinite preciousness."

Subject: I (the descender). Object: black pearl.

BLACK in Hebrew: שָׁחוֹר (Shachor). Shin = 300, Chet = 8, Vav = 6, Resh = 200. Total = 514 = 5 + 1 + 4 = 10 = 1.

PEARL in Hebrew: פְּנִינָה (Pninah). Peh = 80, Nun = 50, Yod = 10, Nun = 50, Heh = 5. Total = 195 = 1 + 9 + 5 = 15 = 6.

Black = 1 (Unity, Kether, Source). Pearl = 6 (Tiphareth, the Son, Beauty, Heart of the Tree). 1 + 6 = 7 = Venus = Magic = Love.

But look deeper. 200 = Resh = the Head. In Sepher Sephiroth, 200 corresponds to the Head (the top, the crown, consciousness), Poverty (emptiness, lack), and Abundance (fullness, overflow).

The Head is Poverty is Abundance.

The verse says "a black pearl of infinite preciousness." Black = 200 = Resh = Poverty. Poverty of infinite preciousness.

The verse says it in English. The Hebrew confirms it underneath. He plucked Poverty from the abyss, and that poverty IS the pearl of infinite preciousness. The nothing that is everything. The emptiness that is fullness. The Zero that contains all numbers.

Two languages. One truth. Two witnesses.

∴

VERSE 65 – THE COMPLETION

Text: "For I have found Thee alike in the Me and the Thee; there is no difference, O my beautiful, my desirable One! In the One and the Many have I found Thee; yea, I have found Thee."

Verse number: 65. Stress count: 15. 65 = 6 + 5 = 11 (Master number, not reduced). 15 = 1 + 5 = 6. 6 + 11 = 17 = 1 + 7 = 8.

8 = ∞ = infinity = the lemniscate.

The final verse of the chapter numbered for Adonai (65) resolves to infinity. Whether this was intentional cannot be determined from the outside. The correspondence is noted.

CONCLUSION

What the analysis suggests: the stress counts appear to encode sephirotic values, the verse numbers participate in the mathematics, verse plus stress combinations correspond to Tarot attributions and Qabalistic meanings and Hebrew names, Hebrew gematria of key words aligns with the English surface meaning, and the same patterns appear at multiple layers simultaneously.

The encoding appears to go deeper than shown here. Multiplication, division, letter-by-letter analysis, and cross-referencing with 777 tables each reveal more.

Good. This is exactly the kind of material that benefits from surgical restraint.

PART THREE:

THE TWELVE AND THE THREE

Structural Analysis

What follows emerged from the verse-by-verse analysis. Upon completion, the 65 verses grouped into twelve sections based on thematic continuity. The divisions were not externally imposed but arose from internal coherence within the text.

A numerical analysis was then performed.

The Twelve Sections

12 sections.

The number twelve corresponds structurally to several traditional symbolic systems, including the Zodiac, the Simple Letters, and the months.

First Calculation

$12 + 40 + 48 = 100$

$1 + 0 + 0 = 1$

The number of sections (12), plus verse 40, plus verse 48, reduces to 1.

Section Reductions

Each section was calculated by adding:

Section number + all verse numbers within that section

The total was reduced to a single digit.

Sequence of reductions:

$2 \rightarrow 4 \rightarrow 6 \rightarrow 8 \rightarrow 5 \rightarrow 6 \rightarrow 7 \rightarrow 1 \rightarrow 9 \rightarrow 8 \rightarrow 7 \rightarrow 3$

Second Calculation

$2 + 4 + 6 + 8 + 5 + 6 + 7 + 1 + 9 + 8 + 7 + 3 = 66$

$6 + 6 = 12$

$1 + 2 = 3$

The cumulative reduction yields 3.

In traditional Kabbalistic attribution, the number 3 corresponds to Binah.

No interpretive claim is made beyond noting the numerical correspondence.

Correspondences

Using the reductions, each section may be mapped to:

- A Sephirah
- A planetary attribution
- A Tarot trump

These mappings follow established symbolic systems.

Third Calculation

The twelve Tarot trumps:

$$0 + 2 + 5 + 10 + 3 + 15 + 16 + 21 + 13 + 12 + 6 + 17 = 120$$
$$1 + 2 + 0 = 3$$

The total reduces to 3.

Across three independent calculations, the final reduction resolves to 3.

This numerical convergence is observed without interpretive assertion.

Structural Observation

The chapter numbered 65 — traditionally associated with the value of *Adonai* — reduces structurally, through multiple independent calculations, to 3.

In Kabbalistic attribution, 3 corresponds to Binah.

The numerical relationship between 65 and 3 is documented here as a structural feature of the analysis. No metaphysical conclusion is drawn.

If the observed pattern is intentional—something that cannot be demonstrated conclusively—then the possibility of deliberate encoding may be considered. It is equally possible that the pattern reflects structural coincidence or apophenic projection. The numerical relationships themselves are verifiable. The interpretive framework applied to them remains my own.

The analytical procedure followed the method commonly referred to as Scientific Illuminism: memorization of the text, prolonged saturation, systematic analysis, and extended periods of non-intervention. The numerical calculations were not selected retroactively to support a conclusion. They were derived from the natural groupings that emerged over years of sustained engagement with the material, after which the arithmetic was applied. The recurrence of specific reductions across independent calculations is documented as a structural feature of the analysis. The symbolic attribution of these reductions, including their correspondence within Kabbalistic systems, reflects a traditional interpretive model rather than a claim of metaphysical disclosure. The presence of the attributed principle within the structure is therefore noted as an interpretive conclusion, not as an objective proof.

CHAPTER THREE:
THE ARGENTUM ASTRUM

The Laboratory That Built the Technology

∴

The previous two chapters presented what I identified as a hidden narrative structure in Liber LXV, Chapter III: a man walking to execution, encoded beneath its traditional mystical reading. The mathematical analysis, as performed, yielded twelve sections resolving to three, the number attributed to Binah in the Kabbalistic system. That result is documented in the preceding chapter. Interpretation remains separate from verification.

A structural finding requires contextual placement. The text emerged from a specific initiatory system with defined methods and instructional discipline. The question, therefore, is what framework produced it and under what assumptions such writing was constructed. My working framework for approaching the material is the Argentum Astrum.

This chapter outlines the system as I understand it based on the primary sources I have studied. I do not claim institutional authority within the A∴A∴. I write as a practitioner who followed the published instructions as I understood them and recorded the outcomes. The observations presented here reflect that position.

∴

The Founding

The A∴A∴—Argentum Astrum, the Silver Star—was established in 1907 by Aleister Crowley and George Cecil Jones following the collapse of the Hermetic Order of the Golden Dawn. The name is traditionally associated with the star Sirius, which appears in various initiatory and symbolic traditions. According to its founding documents, the Order was not presented as a continuation of the Golden Dawn but as a structural reconfiguration. The distinction is explicit in early A∴A∴ materials.

The Golden Dawn functioned as a lodge-based organization with hierarchical officers and committee governance. Advancement occurred through formal initiations, and administrative conflict contributed to its fragmentation. In contrast, the A∴A∴ was structured as a sequence of individual instructional relationships: one student working with one instructor, who in turn answered to another superior. The model reduced collective governance in favor of direct transmission.

There were no lodges or committee structures within the formal design. The architecture appears intended to minimize the internal political dynamics that affected its predecessor. Whether this structural decision originated primarily with Crowley, Jones, or their collaboration cannot be determined with certainty. It may be observed, however, that the model directly addresses identifiable weaknesses within the Golden Dawn framework.

The Axioms

The philosophical foundation is stated in two phrases that serve as greeting and closing of official correspondence: "Do what thou wilt shall be the whole of the Law." "Love is the law, love under will." These statements originate in *Liber AL vel Legis* (The Book of the Law) and are treated within the system as axiomatic. They are not framed as moral exhortations but as doctrinal propositions concerning human purpose.

Within the tradition, the first phrase is interpreted as asserting the existence of a True Will, defined as an essential course of action aligned with a larger order. The discovery and execution of that Will is described as the central Work of the system. The second phrase qualifies the first by defining love as the operational mode of that Will. These interpretations reflect established internal commentaries rather than personal innovation.

Love, in this context, is defined not as sentiment but as the union of subject and object. It is described as the resolution of duality through directed action. The language is technical within the symbolic vocabulary of the system. This is the interpretive framework I brought to the practice, while recognizing that other readings exist.

The Three Orders

The A∴A∴ is divided into three bodies, each corresponding to a defined section of the Qabalistic Tree of Life. The grade system maps symbolically onto the Sephiroth and establishes a sequential progression of work. Each grade carries prescribed practices, examinations, and doctrinal expectations. The structure is explicit in the published materials of the Order.

Order of the Golden Dawn (G∴D∴)
Outer College

Grades: Student through Philosophus ($4°=7°$)
Sephiroth: Malkuth, Yesod, Hod, Netzach
Primary Work: Elemental mastery and preparatory discipline

This order corresponds to the lower Sephiroth and focuses on foundational training. The work is structured around mastery of the four classical elements and the stabilization of practice. Advancement proceeds through examination and supervision within the instructional chain. The emphasis is preparatory rather than culminatory.

Order of the Rosy Cross (R∴C∴)
Second Order
Grades: Adept Minor ($5°=6°$), Adept Major ($6°=5°$), Adept Exemptus ($7°=4°$)
Sephiroth: Tiphareth, Geburah, Chesed
Primary Work: Knowledge and Conversation of the Holy Guardian Angel and integration of attainment

This order corresponds to the central Sephiroth and is associated with the attainment termed the Knowledge and Conversation of the Holy Guardian Angel. The task is described as both realization and integration of that experience into practical life. The grade structure reflects increasing responsibility and doctrinal depth. The language used to describe this stage remains internal to the system's metaphysical vocabulary.

Order of the Silver Star (S∴S∴)
Third Order
Grades: Magister Templi ($8°=3°$), Magus ($9°=2°$), Ipsissimus ($10°=1°$)
Sephiroth: Binah, Chokmah, Kether

Requirement: Crossing of the Abyss as defined within A∴A∴ doctrine

This order corresponds to the Supernal Triad and represents the highest grades within the formal structure. Entry is described as requiring the crossing of the Abyss, defined in system literature as a dissolution of the constructed ego-identity. The symbolic attainment associated with this transition is the City of the Pyramids. These descriptions follow the terminology of the primary documents.

The grade system maps directly to the Tree of Life, providing a symbolic architecture for progression. Each grade has defined correspondences, prescribed practices, and evaluative standards. The Tree functions as an organizing framework rather than a metaphor alone. This structural coherence was one factor that drew me to the system, though no comparative claim is advanced beyond that observation.

The Grade System

The notation follows the formula $X°=Y°$. The first number indicates the grade within the Order. The second indicates the corresponding Sephirah, counted from Malkuth upward. This dual notation situates each grade simultaneously within the institutional hierarchy and the symbolic architecture of the Tree of Life.

Student
Preliminary status prior to admission
Requirement: pass an examination demonstrating familiarity with

foundational texts
Minimum period: three months

Required study includes *The Equinox*, *Liber* 777, the *Collected Works of Aleister Crowley*, *Raja Yoga* by Swami Vivekananda, the *Tao Teh King*, and Éliphas Lévi's *Transcendental Magic*, among others. The emphasis is intellectual preparation before formal entry. The examination functions as a threshold rather than an initiation. The period of study is specified as no less than three months.

Probationer (0°=0°)
Task: begin a Magical Record and practice the basic methods for one year
Requirement: obtain thorough intellectual knowledge of the system
Memorization: one chapter of *Liber LXV*

This grade marks formal entry into the work. The keeping of a Magical Record is mandatory and functions as both discipline and documentation. The one-year period establishes continuity of practice. Memorization of a chapter of *Liber LXV* is specified in the published curriculum.

Neophyte (1°=10°)
Sephirah: Malkuth (Earth)
Primary Text: *Liber E*
Implements: Earth Pantacle

The practices include record-keeping, tests of clairvoyance, Asana, Pranayama, and Dharana. The focus is stabilization and control at the level symbolically attributed to Earth. In my experience, the difficulty of this grade derived less from technical complexity than from the absence of accumulated momentum. The work establishes baseline discipline rather than culmination.

Zelator (2°=9°)
Sephirah: Yesod (Air)
Primary Text: *Liber RV*
Implements: Air Dagger

The grade emphasizes Pranayama and breath control, including nine distinct breathing practices. The text instructs: "Let the Zelator breathe as deeply and rapidly as possible." The stated objective is control of Prana through regulated respiration. The discipline is technical and repetitive.

Practicus (3°=8°)
Sephirah: Hod (Water)
Primary Focus: Mantra Yoga
Implements: Water Cup

The work centers on the use of sound and vibration as operative tools. Mantra is treated as a technical instrument rather than devotional expression. The symbolic attribution aligns with Water and its associative qualities within the system. The grade continues the structured progression through the elemental schema.

Philosophus (4°=7°)
Sephirah: Netzach (Fire)
Primary Text: *Liber Astarte*
Implements: Fire Wand

The work involves Bhakti Yoga, defined as union through devotion. This grade completes the elemental cycle established in the Outer College. The emphasis shifts toward directed emotional and symbolic intensity within controlled parameters. The structure presents this as culmination of the elemental sequence.

Dominus Liminis
Designation: The Portal
Symbolism: The Veil of Paroketh

This grade functions as a transitional threshold between the First and Second Orders. The title translates as "Lord of the Threshold." It marks a liminal position rather than a Sephirothic attribution. The symbolism emphasizes passage rather than attainment.

Adeptus Minor ($5°=6°$)
Sephirah: Tiphareth (Sun)
Primary Text: *Liber Samekh*
Designation: "Crown of the Outer College"

This grade is defined by the attainment termed the Knowledge and Conversation of the Holy Guardian Angel. The literature describes it as the central attainment toward which the preliminary grades orient. The symbolic attribution to the Sun reflects this centrality within the Tree. The practices are structured accordingly.

Adeptus Major ($6°=5°$)
Sephirah: Geburah (Mars)

The grade is described in system texts as mastery of magick in its forms, though without complete comprehension. The aspirant is directed toward persistence in preparation for the Abyss. The attribution to Mars reflects severity and discipline within the symbolic framework. Advancement remains structured and supervised.

Adeptus Exemptus (7°=4°)
Sephirah: Chesed (Jupiter)
Task: compose a thesis of the universe

The aspirant is required to condense accumulated knowledge into a single coherent volume. *Liber* 474 prescribes philosophical problems to be examined without recourse to magick or meditation. The instruction states: "He must not seek any refuge from his intellect." The emphasis is analytical consolidation rather than visionary expansion.

Babe of the Abyss
Designation: The Crossing
Primary Text: *Liber Cheth vel Vallum Abiegni*

This stage describes the passage between the phenomenal world and the Supernal Triad. The Abyss contains Choronzon, characterized as the force of dispersion, and the false Sephirah Da'ath. The crossing is defined as surrender of all attachments, including identity constructs. The language is symbolic and doctrinal.

Magister Templi (8°=3°)
Sephirah: Binah (Saturn)

This grade is associated with the Great Sea and the City of the Pyramids. The Magister Templi is described as tending the Garden within system literature. The attribution aligns with

Binah in the Supernal Triad. The symbolism emphasizes containment and structure.

Magus (9°=2°)
Sephirah: Chokmah

The Magus is described as attaining the Word and being obligated to utter it. The doctrine includes the so-called "Curse of the Grade," defined as the creative and destructive power of speech. The attribution corresponds to Chokmah within the Tree. The language remains symbolic and internal to the tradition.

Ipsissimus (10°=1°)
Sephirah: Kether

This grade is described as beyond formulation. The published materials state that nothing can meaningfully be said of it. The attribution aligns with Kether, the crown. The description remains deliberately minimal.

I have not attained the higher grades described above. The descriptions provided here are drawn from published materials rather than personal experience. Where experiential commentary appears in earlier grades, it is identified as such. The remainder reflects textual summary.

✦ ✦ ✦
The Classification of Texts

A∴A∴ publications are classified by stated authority. The classification system is internal to the Order and determines how a text is to be approached in practice. The categories distinguish between doctrinal status and practical instruction. The hierarchy is explicit in official documents.

Class A — Holy Books. Written in a state described as illumination and to be accepted without alteration or commentary. The tradition maintains that such texts come through the author rather than originating from them.

Class B — Books useful for study but representing the opinion of the author.

Class C — Books suggestive but neither authoritative nor philosophical.

Class D — Official rituals and instructions.

Class E — Public manifestos and broadsheets.

This classification affects practical engagement with the material. The category assigned to a text determines the degree of interpretive latitude permitted within the system. Liber LXV, analyzed in Chapters One and Two, is designated Class A. According to the tradition, it is said to have come through Crowley rather than from him; whether that claim is accurate cannot be demonstrated, though my experience has not contradicted it.

✦ ✦ ✦

Personal Perspective

Based on my reading of the instructions, the method consists of five components. The first is memorization: commit the text to exact internal recall, preserving wording and sequence without paraphrase. The second is saturation: sustained exposure over extended time until the material becomes structurally embedded rather than merely studied. The third is analysis: application of the system's technical tools, including gematria, correspondence tables such as *Liber* 777, scansion, and cross-reference. The fourth is recording, defined as systematic documentation in a Magical Record. The fifth is examination, requiring demonstration of attainment prior to advancement rather than reliance on self-report.

This summary reflects how I interpreted the published instructions. The sequence is procedural rather than symbolic. Each component reinforces the others. Alternative interpretations of emphasis or sequence are possible.

What Came Before

Chapters One and Two document the outcome of applying this method to *Liber LXV*, Chapter III. Memorization was completed years prior to formal analysis. Saturation consisted of extended internal recitation over approximately nine years. Analysis involved verse-by-verse scansion, stress patterns, gematria, and Tarot correspondences, with results documented in written form.

The narrative interpretation—the figure walking toward execution—emerged during saturation rather than during deliberate analysis. It was not constructed through conscious planning but appeared after prolonged internalization of the text. The subsequent numerical analysis produced a structural pattern: twelve sections resolving to three. The arithmetic was performed after the divisions had been established, not as a retroactive justification.

Both the narrative emergence and the numerical convergence are presented as outcomes of applying the prescribed method. The data are reproducible at the level of calculation. The interpretive layer remains mine. I conclude that the text contains structural features that become apparent when approached through the system's stated procedures.

Based on this experience, the A∴A∴ system presents a defined curriculum, a structured grade hierarchy, prescribed practices documented in Class D texts, examination standards, and a model of individual transmission. The primary source materials are publicly available. Whether this structure constitutes superiority over other systems is not asserted. I report that when I followed the instructions as I understood them, observable results followed.

"Do what thou wilt shall be the whole of the Law."
"Love is the law, love under will."

CHAPTER FOUR:
A STONE ON THE PATH
Conclusion

This study began with a procedural question: what occurs when a text described as initiatory technology is subjected to the method it prescribes. The method was not constructed for this project but is embedded in the A∴A∴ curriculum: memorize the text, saturate consciousness with it, record observations, analyze correspondences, and wait. The instruction assumes that results follow sustained attention rather than belief. This book documents the outcomes observed when that procedure was applied.

The Traditional Reading Remains Valid

The traditional interpretation of *Liber LXV*, Chapter III—aspirant below, Angel above, movement toward union—has remained consistent within the A∴A∴ corpus for more than a century. It aligns with Crowley's commentaries and with the broader initiatory structure of the system. That reading is not displaced here. The alternative reading presented alongside it operates on a different axis rather than in opposition.

The horizontal reading—a man walking toward execution, a beloved woman already dead, a seal broken between worlds—emerged after prolonged internal recitation. It did not negate the established vertical structure. The text appears capable of sustaining both readings simultaneously. That dual capacity is recorded as an observed feature rather than as an evaluative claim.

The Zero Formula

In *Alchemy Reimagined*, I proposed that zero functions not as absence but as a generative baseline from which polarity emerges. From zero, positive and negative values arise, producing oscillation when plotted. Zero is not inert within mathematical systems; it permits relation and return. The analogy is structural rather than metaphorical.

A comparable structural principle appears in *Liber LXV*, Chapter III. The chapter numbered 65—traditionally associated with Adonai—reduces through documented calculations to 3, attributed in Kabbalistic systems to Binah. The numerical reduction is verifiable. The symbolic correspondence follows established attribution tables.

The twelve structural divisions of the chapter, when summed and reduced, resolve to 3. The twelve Tarot correspondences assigned in analysis, when summed and reduced, also resolve to 3. Independent calculations yield the same reduction. The connection to Binah and its associated symbolic field is noted as a pattern observed within that framework.

Whether the structure was intentionally embedded, whether it arises from unconscious composition, or whether it reflects interpretive projection cannot be demonstrated conclusively. The arithmetic is reproducible. The symbolic attribution follows tradition. The interpretation remains provisional.

This study records what was done and what was found. The conclusions are limited to structural observation and documented correspondence. No further claim is advanced.

The One Who Notices

I once sat on a meditation mat in a temple in Ukiah, California, under the assumption that I was meditating. A monk approached and stood beside me. He said, "You're sitting on a meditation mat." I answered, "Yes." He replied, "You're not meditating."

The statement was direct and accurate. I acknowledged that prior attempts at meditation had consisted largely of effortful attempts to silence thought, which had not succeeded. Silence and sustained mental stillness had remained inconsistent. My approach had been structured around suppression.

He responded that the difficulty arose from the premise. If the objective is to eliminate thought entirely, the effort will fail. Thought continues as a function of consciousness. It does not cease on command.

He then reframed the task. Rather than attempting to suppress thought, he suggested observing it. Thoughts continue whether or not one participates in them. Recognition of this distinction alters the relationship to mental activity.

He concluded that meditation is not the forced silencing of thoughts but the recognition of the one who notices them. The emphasis is on awareness rather than suppression. The distinction is procedural rather than mystical. It shifts the locus of practice from content to observation.

This is how I understand the underlying instruction of A∴A∴ work. The emphasis is not accumulation of knowledge but recognition of the knower. The texts function as instruments rather than conclusions. The correspondences are tools for attention rather than objects of belief.

Crowley states in *Magick in Theory and Practice* (1929/1997, Ch. I), "The first condition of success in Magic is therefore the ability to control thought; to still the mind, to concentrate it upon a single idea." In practical terms, control does not require suppression. It requires disciplined relationship to mental process. The operative movement is recognition of the one who notices.

The Work

The documents exist and are publicly accessible. The procedural outline is explicit in the instructions: memorize, saturate, analyze, wait. The structure does not depend on institutional permission or formal recognition. It depends on execution. The burden of proof rests in application.

The stress patterns are present in the verses. The gematria is embedded in the language. The correspondences are catalogued in *Liber* 777, which is available in print and digital form. The chapter numbered 65 reduces to 3 through documented calculation. The symbolic attribution follows established tables; the arithmetic is straightforward.

Contemporary tools alter the practical landscape. Search functions, digital archives, and computational software reduce the time required for cross-reference and verification. Materials that once required physical access can now be obtained rapidly. The accessibility of the corpus removes logistical barriers but does not eliminate procedural demands.

Reports in medical and physiological literature describing synchrony, coherence, and entrainment in cardiac and neural activity should not be dismissed as measurement artifacts. Such phenomena may indicate dynamics not yet fully modeled within existing frameworks. Whether these patterns require revised theoretical structures remains an open question. The data warrant examination without premature conclusion.

An Invitation

This book is not a manifesto or a claim of authority. It is a record of one practitioner applying a prescribed method to prescribed material over an extended period and analyzing the results with the tools indicated by the system. The conclusions are limited to documented outcomes and interpretive inferences drawn from them. No broader claim is asserted.

The traditional reading of Chapter III remains intact. The alternative reading presented here is offered as a complementary structure rather than a replacement. Both interpretations may coexist within the same textual architecture. In my experience, the vertical reading presents first; the horizontal structure emerged after prolonged internalization.

Different readers may derive different structures from the same material. This variability reflects interaction between operator and system rather than doctrinal instability. The A∴A∴ functions as a procedural framework rather than a belief system. Outcomes are shaped by duration of engagement, methodological consistency, and quality of documentation.

The texts remain available for examination. Their structure does not depend on urgency. The work proceeds at the pace of application.

"The master has failed more times than the student has tried."

93 93/93
Frater Lachesis Peyton o°=o A∴A∴

CHAPTER FIVE:
THE MIRROR AND THE STAR
Jack Parsons, the Edge We All Walk, and One Star in Sight

✦ ✦ ✦

John Whiteside Parsons died in 1952 in an explosion at his home laboratory in Pasadena, California. The official report described the cause as an accidental detonation involving fulminate of mercury. Alternative interpretations have been proposed over the years, including suicide and foul play, though no conclusive evidence has displaced the accident ruling. The circumstances of his death remain part of the historical record and subsequent speculation.

Parsons was a co-founder of what became the Jet Propulsion Laboratory and a key figure in early American rocketry. Largely self-taught, he contributed to the development of solid rocket propellants and published research that advanced propulsion science. His work helped establish the technical foundations later used in the American space program. Within his research group at the California Institute of Technology, hazardous experimentation led colleagues to refer to themselves informally as the "Suicide Squad."

In parallel with his scientific work, Parsons was an active practitioner of ceremonial magic within the Thelemic tradition. His engagement was not peripheral; he held leadership roles and conducted organized ritual work. He approached occult practice with the same seriousness he applied to engineering problems.

For him, both domains involved structured procedure and disciplined experimentation.

Parsons operated from the premise that consciousness could exert causal influence under defined conditions. He treated ritual as a functional system rather than symbolic theater. Whether his conclusions were justified remains a matter of interpretation. His life illustrates an attempt to pursue scientific and esoteric inquiry simultaneously, without compartmentalization.

The Man

Parsons was born in 1914 in Los Angeles. By early adulthood he was conducting rocket experiments with collaborators who would later formalize their work into the Jet Propulsion Laboratory. He lacked a formal university degree but educated himself through independent study and experimentation. His persistence contributed to the transition of rocketry from speculative pursuit to applied science.

He encountered Thelema in his twenties and became affiliated with the Ordo Templi Orientis. By the early 1940s he was leading the Agape Lodge in Pasadena. Ritual activity occurred in the same residence where he conducted propulsion experiments. He did not treat these domains as contradictory; he regarded both as technical systems requiring precision and discipline.

Aleister Crowley corresponded with Parsons and commented on his activities in surviving letters. Crowley expressed admiration for Parsons' intellect while also noting concern regarding his intensity and judgment. Parsons was described in correspondence as a highly valued member of the Order in America. The documentary record reflects both recognition and caution.

The Working

In January 1946, Jack Parsons initiated a series of ritual operations later referred to as the Babalon Working. The stated objective was to invoke and incarnate Babalon, a figure in Thelemic symbolism associated with liberated feminine force. Parsons framed the operation against the backdrop of the recently concluded war and the deployment of atomic weapons, which he interpreted as indicators of destructive imbalance. His proposed corrective was ritual intervention.

The operations incorporated Enochian material derived from the system recorded by John Dee and Edward Kelley in the sixteenth century. They also incorporated sexual ritual techniques transmitted within the O.T.O. Parsons conducted the work over several weeks and maintained written records of procedures and perceived results. These records describe environmental disturbances and subjective phenomena.

During this period, Marjorie Cameron entered Parsons' life. Parsons interpreted her arrival as connected to the working. The causal relationship cannot be demonstrated; the sequence of events is documented. Shortly thereafter, L. Ron Hubbard became directly involved in Parsons' activities.

The Scandal

Marjorie Cameron was an artist who later became associated with the California occult milieu. Parsons regarded her as the elemental counterpart invoked in his ritual work. Whether this interpretation reflects symbolic projection or coincidence remains undetermined. The documented fact is that their relationship began during the period of the Babalon Working.

L. Ron Hubbard, then a science fiction writer, was present at the Agape Lodge and participated in ritual sessions as a recorder. During this period, Hubbard began a relationship with Betty, who had been Parsons' partner. The personal and financial entanglements that followed are documented in correspondence and legal filings.

Parsons, Hubbard, and Betty formed a business venture called Allied Enterprises. Parsons invested approximately $50,000 in 1946 currency to purchase yachts for resale. Hubbard and Betty departed with a yacht and funds; Parsons pursued legal action and recovered a portion of the investment. Correspondence from Crowley during this period reflects disapproval of the situation.

Parsons' security clearance was later revoked. Contributing factors included his associations, his public identification with occult practice, and broader postwar scrutiny. His employment became unstable, and he undertook various forms of contract work. On June 17, 1952, an explosion occurred at his home laboratory; he died from injuries sustained. He was thirty-seven years old.

What the Scandal Reveals

The historical record indicates that Parsons' financial and professional decline followed interpersonal and business decisions rather than ritual procedure alone. Hubbard's actions materially affected Parsons' finances and reputation. Parsons appears to have misjudged character and risk within ordinary human dealings. There is no evidence that ritual practice provided protection against those misjudgments.

Engagement in esoteric work did not substitute for practical discernment. The documented events show vulnerability to exploitation independent of metaphysical claims. The pattern illustrates the coexistence of high technical competence in one domain with poor judgment in another. The contrast is observable in the record.

The case does not establish whether the ritual operations were effective in any metaphysical sense. It does establish that human factors determined much of the outcome. The historical sequence can be explained without recourse to supernatural causation. Any additional interpretation remains speculative.

The Question Raised

The Babalon Working took place in 1946. Subsequent decades saw significant cultural shifts related to sexuality, gender roles, and social structure in Western societies. These developments included expanded public discourse on sexuality, legal changes affecting reproductive rights, and increased female participation in professional life. The temporal sequence is factual.

No causal link between Parsons' ritual activity and broader historical change can be demonstrated. Correlation alone does not establish mechanism. The question of symbolic correspondence may be raised, but it remains interpretive rather than evidentiary. Historical movements arise from complex social, economic, and political forces.

It is therefore not possible to conclude that the working produced measurable societal effects. The speculation that it did is part of occult historiography rather than verifiable history. The documented facts remain limited to Parsons' actions, records, relationships, and death. Further claims exceed the available evidence.

The Mirror

Parsons' life has often been framed as a cautionary narrative: a talented engineer diverted into occult speculation, whose private pursuits undermined his public achievements. That framing reduces a complex figure to caricature. The historical record shows a man who applied experimental seriousness to multiple domains. Whether his conclusions were valid is separate from the fact that he pursued them methodically.

He treated ritual practice as something to be tested and documented rather than merely believed. His surviving journals indicate sustained effort and procedural repetition. The question is not whether he was intelligent or sincere; both are well established. The question is whether his application of risk, judgment, and interpretation remained proportionate to the domains he entered.

Much of Parsons' magical work appears to have been conducted without continuous external oversight. Correspondence with Crowley existed but was limited by distance and circumstance. The Agape Lodge functioned as a local body but did not provide structured, long-term evaluative supervision comparable to formal scientific peer review. Parsons appears to have operated with substantial autonomy.

Autonomy in experimental contexts increases both innovation and exposure to error. Without structured counterbalance, confirmation bias and overextension become harder to detect. The historical sequence suggests that personal desire and symbolic interpretation sometimes overlapped in his decisions. That overlap is observable in his writings and subsequent actions.

The Babalon Working, as documented, combined ritual intention with personal relational expectation. When events aligned with expectation, they were interpreted within the ritual framework. When outcomes destabilized, the framework did not mitigate material consequences. The episode illustrates how symbolic systems can intersect with personal motivations.

Any structured discipline—scientific or esoteric—requires internal and external checks. Procedures, staged advancement, documentation, and review function as stabilizing mechanisms in technical fields. Where such mechanisms are absent or informal, variance increases. Parsons' trajectory reflects both high capability and high variance.

The contrast between collective initiation models and individually structured progression systems has been debated within esoteric communities. That debate falls outside verifiable history. What can be stated is that Parsons' work unfolded within a particular organizational environment, and that environment shaped his context. Whether a different structure would have altered outcomes cannot be demonstrated.

The Acknowledgement

Parsons committed himself fully to propositions most of his contemporaries regarded as fringe or untenable. He invested his professional reputation, finances, and personal stability in the integration of scientific and esoteric inquiry. That level of commitment is historically documented. The outcome was not successful in conventional terms.

He treated questions about consciousness and causation as testable rather than symbolic. He was incorrect in several judgments, particularly in matters of trust and risk management. However, the willingness to test a hypothesis at personal cost is not, in itself, evidence of irrationality. It is evidence of conviction.

His life illustrates both ambition and consequence. The same intensity that drove innovation in rocketry was applied to ritual practice and personal decisions. The results included technical achievement and material loss. The pattern is visible in the record.

I refer to his example not as endorsement but as context. Engaging unconventional inquiry carries reputational and social cost. That cost is not abstract. It affects professional standing, relationships, and credibility. These risks are observable in Parsons' case.

The possibility of error remains present in any such undertaking. Historical awareness does not eliminate exposure to misjudgment. It can, however, encourage procedural caution. Parsons' trajectory demonstrates that commitment alone does not guarantee stability.

The Continuation

This book concludes one phase of inquiry rather than closing the subject. The questions raised here extend beyond a single text or analysis. Further examination will address the intersection of language, cognition, and disciplined practice. The objective is documentation rather than proclamation.

Future work will examine the interaction between symbolic systems and neurological process, using language as operational variable. The intent is analytical, not devotional. Historical traditions will be evaluated as structured methods rather than as belief systems. Comparative material will be treated descriptively.

The example of Parsons remains relevant as historical data. His failures do not invalidate all inquiry; they illustrate points of instability. Risk assessment is part of disciplined exploration. Observation replaces romanticization.

Continuation does not imply escalation. It implies sustained method. Any conclusions will remain provisional and subject to revision. The work proceeds incrementally.

One Star in Sight

This concludes the fifth chapter of this book. The sequence was not pre-planned; the structure developed during composition. The chapters organized into five thematic movements: system, path, method, reflection, and conclusion. The recurrence of five is noted as a structural feature.

Within Western esoteric symbolism, five is traditionally associated with the microcosm and the pentagram. The figure of the human body extended in five points is a common representation. These associations are part of established symbolic vocabulary. They are referenced here descriptively.

Liber LXV, Chapter III, when subjected to numerical reduction, produces the following sequence: $65 + 3 = 68; 6 + 8 = 14; 1 + 4 = 5$. The arithmetic is straightforward. The reduction yields 5. The result is recorded without extending its implication.

The name "Elyalith," previously referenced, also reduces to five under standard gematric calculation. The calculation is reproducible. The correspondence between chapter structure and name value is therefore noted. Interpretation is withheld pending broader context.

Crowley titled a foundational A∴A∴ document "One Star in Sight." The phrase refers to the individual aspirant rather than a collective constellation. The metaphor emphasizes singular orientation. The title situates the individual within a symbolic field rather than dissolving identity into abstraction.

The opening lines of that document describe disorientation and obscurity, followed by a shift toward recognition. The pivot emphasizes the persistence of individual identity within larger structure. The imagery is poetic but structurally consistent with the system's focus on singular development. The reference is included as historical context rather than doctrinal assertion.

APPENDIX

Methodological Note

I will do only one verse in full as a demonstration.

What follows is a complete comparative gematria and Kabbalistic analysis of a single verse, performed twice: once using the operational English-letter method developed in this book, and once using traditional Hebrew Kabbalah with its standard gematria systems.

The operational English method (A=1···Z=26) follows the approach described throughout this work—treating letters as numerical values, separating subject/object/predicate structures, and applying arithmetic operations to reveal relational patterns. The traditional Hebrew analysis employs the classical methods: Mispar Hechrechi (absolute value), Mispar Katan (digit reduction), Mispar Siduri (ordinal position), Milui (spelling-out), Atbash (letter reversal), and Albam (half-alphabet substitution).

Whether done my way or done traditionally, the numbers speak for themselves. The purpose of running both systems on the same verse is not to prove equivalence or claim hidden meaning. It is to test structural invariance under transformation—to see whether relational topology persists when the same semantic content passes through independent symbolic frameworks. Where convergence occurs, it indicates stable reception dynamics rather than encoded

content. Where breaks occur, they are equally informative. Nothing in what follows requires belief. Everything can be repeated. The mathematics function as diagnostics of fidelity, not carriers of meaning.

The Twelve Sections

§	Verses	Theme	Red.	Tarot	Sephirah
I	1-4	Entry & The Three Fates	2	0 — Fool	Chokmah
2	5-10	The Beloved & The Taint	4	II — Priestess	Chesed
3	11-16	Grief, Prayer, Gods Arrive	6	V — Hierophant	Tiphareth
4	17-20	The Snake of Emerald	8	X — Wheel	Hod
5	21-24	The First Death	5	III — Empress	Geburah
6	25-31	After the First Death	6	XV — Devil	Tiphareth
7	32-39	The Second Death	7	XVI — Tower	Netzach
8	40-48	The Third Death	1	XXI — Universe	Kether
9	49-54	Transformation & Rebirth	9	XIII — Death	Yesod
10	55-58	The Accusation	8	XII — Hanged Man	Hod
11	59-62	The Drop	7	VI — Lovers	Netzach
12	63-65	The Black Pearl	3	XVII — Star	Binah

The Three Proofs

First Proof: 12 + 40 + 48 = 100 = 1 + 0 + 0 = 1 (Unity, Kether)

Second Proof: 2+4+6+8+5+6+7+1+9+8+7+3 = 66 = 12 = 3 (Binah)

Third Proof: 0+2+5+10+3+15+16+21+13+12+6+17 = 120 = 3 (Binah)

Complete Stress Count Table

V	First Words	Str	V+S	Red
1	Verily and Amen! I passed...	13	14	5
2	Wherein was a white unicorn...	10	12	3
3	Then the word of Adonai...	16	19	1
4	But I remembered. Yea, Than...	10	14	5
5	Beautiful wast thou, O Lilith...	6	11	11
6	Thou wast lithe and delicious...	7	13	4
7	Close didst thou cling...	7	14	5
8	But I beheld in thee a taint...	6	14	5
9	I beheld in thee the taint...	9	18	9

10	I gazed upon the Crystal...	7	17	8
11	Further, I destroyed the time...	8	19	1
12	But in the very hour...	4	16	7
13	Then I said: O my beloved...	8	21	3
14	But she was closed fast...	6	20	2
15	Also I prayed unto the Elephant...	7	22	4
16	These gods came right quickly...	9	25	7
17	Then I beheld myself compassed...	7	24	6
18	O Snake of Emerald, Thou hast...	9	27	9
19	Thou art delicious beyond...	19	38	11
20	Also Thy coils are of infinite...	7	27	9
21	I, and Me, and Mine were sitting...	11	32	5

22	The night fell, and the music...	5	27	9
23	The tempest arose, and the music...	5	28	1
24	The hour passed, and the music...	5	29	11
25	But Thou art Eternity and Space...	7	32	5
26	For there is no Symbol of Thee.	2	28	1
27	If I say Come up upon...	10	37	1
28	The red three-angled heart...	10	38	11
29	Yet all the while Thou wast...	7	36	9
30	Thou art Sebek the crocodile...	21	51	6
31	I turned me about thrice...	8	39	3
32	Many things I beheld mediate...	9	41	5
33	Come thou, O beloved One...	11	44	8

34	All day I sing of Thy delight...	6	40	4
35	There is no other day or night...	4	39	3
36	Thou art beyond the day...	7	43	7
37	I am like the little red dog...	6	43	7
38	Thou hast brought me into great...	9	47	11
39	Thou hast fastened the fangs...	8	47	11
40	I am become like a luscious...	19	59	5
41	She hath slain her kinsfolk...	8	49	4
42	She hath been broken in pieces...	7	49	4
43	The fountains of water have been...	6	49	4
44	She hath burst in sunder...	7	51	6
45	So am I, O Adonai, my lord...	5	50	5

46	So am I, O Adonai, my beloved...	5	51	6
47	I am shed out like spilt blood...	9	56	11
48	Therefore is the seal unloosed...	12	60	6
49	Yea, also verily Thou art...	9	58	4
50	That which went in as a brave...	11	61	7
51	O Thou light and delight...	7	58	4
52	O Thou Son of a light-transcending...	9	61	7
53	Behold! I am a butterfly...	9	62	8
54	Also the stream of the stars...	9	63	9
55	This is the world of the waters...	15	70	7
56	I follow Thee, and the waters...	11	67	4
57	How shall I answer the foolish...	7	64	1

58	But I am the Fool that heedeth...	13	71	8
59	Therefore is the Eagle made one...	9	68	5
60	I have descended, O my darling...	11	71	8
61	I have gone down, O my God...	11	72	9
62	But as Thou art the Last...	6	68	5
63	They that ever desired Thee...	6	69	6
64	Glorious, glorious, glorious...	7	71	8
65	For I have found Thee alike...	15	80	8

Notable Patterns

Verse 26 ("For there is no Symbol of Thee"): 2 stresses — the lowest, closest to zero.

Verse 30 (Typhon/Python): 21 stresses — the highest, maximum expansion.

Verses 22-24 (Three Stillings): All have exactly 5 stresses.

Verse 65 (Completion): Reduces to 8 — infinity, the lemniscate.

Liber 777 – Alchemical Correspondences

Table I – The Four Elements

Attribute	Fire	Water	Air	Earth
Glyph	🜂	🜄	🜁	🜃
Qualities	Hot, Dry	Cold, Moist	Hot, Moist	Cold, Dry
Operation	Calcination	Dissolution	Sublimation	Coagulation
Planet	☉	☽	☿	♄
Tarot	XX Judgement	II Priestess	I Magus	XXI Universe

Table II – Tria Prima (Three Principles)

Attribute	Sulphur	Mercury	Salt
Glyph	🜍	☿	🜔
Classical Term	Soul	Spirit	Body
Quality	Active	Passive	Fixed
Operation	Fermentation	Distillation	Fixation
Planet	☉	☿	♄
Tarot	XI Lust	I Magus	XIV Art

Table III – Alchemical Operations

Operation	Governing Force	Glyph
Calcination	Fire	🜂
Dissolution	Water	🜄
Sublimation	Air	🜁
Coagulation	Earth	🜃
Fermentation	Sulphur	🜍
Distillation	Mercury	☿
Fixation	Salt	🜔

Full Comparative Gematria Analysis

Liber LXV, Chapter III, Verse 64 (Operational English Method + Traditional Hebrew Kabbalah)

I. Source Text

"Glorious, glorious, glorious art Thou, O my lover supernal, O Self of myself."

מפואר מפואר מפואר אתה אהובי עליון עצמי מעצמי

Table I: Source Verse

Language	Text
English	Glorious, glorious, glorious art Thou, O my lover supernal, O Self of myself.
Hebrew	מפואר מפואר מפואר אתה אהובי עליון עצמי מעצמי

II. Operational English Method (A1Z26)

Letter Values: A=1, B=2 ... Z=26. Spaces and punctuation ignored.

Payload words: GLORIOUS ×3, LOVER, SUPERNAL, SELF, MYSELF. Payload count: 7 words.

Table II: English Word Values

Word	Calculation	Total
GLORIOUS	$G_7+L_{12}+O_{15}+R_{18}+I_9+O_{15}+U_{21}+S_{19}$	116
(×3)	116×3	348
LOVER	$L_{12}+O_{15}+V_{22}+E_5+R_{18}$	72
SUPERNAL	$S_{19}+U_{21}+P_{16}+E_5+R_{18}+N_{14}+A_1+L_{12}$	106
SELF	$S_{19}+E_5+L_{12}+F_6$	42
MYSELF	$M_{13}+Y_{25}+S_{19}+E_5+L_{12}+F_6$	80
PAYLOAD	$348+72+106+42+80$	648

Reduction: $6+4+8 = 18 \rightarrow 9$

III. Subject / Object / Predicate Separation

Table 3: Structural Summary

Component	Words	Raw	Reduced
Subject (Identity)	SELF + MYSELF	122	5
Object (Beloved)	LOVER + SUPERNAL	178	7
Predicate (Charge)	GLORIOUS ×3	348	6
Payload Total		648	9

IV. Arithmetic Operations

Subject $\leftrightarrow$ Object

Add: $122 + 178 = 300 \rightarrow 3$

Subtract: $|178 - 122| = 56 \rightarrow 11$ (structurally significant: $5+6=11$)

Multiply: $122 \times 178 = 21716 \rightarrow 17 \rightarrow 8$

Divide: $178/122 \approx 1.459$; $122/178 \approx 0.685$

Predicate Interactions

Predicate + Subject = 348 + 122 = 470 → 11

Predicate + Object = 348 + 178 = 526 → 13 → 4

Predicate − Subject = 226 → 10 → 1

Predicate − Object = 170 → 8

Predicate × Subject = 42456 → 21 → 3

Predicate × Object = 61944 → 24 → 6

Full Verse (All Words Included)

Including function words: Total = 840 → 12 → 3

V. Traditional Hebrew Kabbalah

Hebrew Translation (for Calculation):

מפואר מפואר מפואר אתה אהובי עליון עצמי מעצמי

VI. Mispar Hechrechi (Standard Gematria)

Table 4: Hebrew Letter Values

Letter	Value	Letter	Value	Letter	Value
ק	100	י	10	א	1
ר	200	כ/ך	20	ב	2
ש	300	ל	30	ג	3
ת	400	מ/ם	40	ד	4
נ/ן	50	ה	5		
ס	60	ו	6		
ע	70	ז	7		
פ/ף	80	ח	8		
צ/ץ	90	ט	9		

Table V: Word-by-Word Gematria — Mispar Hechrechi

Word	Hebrew	Calculation	Total
Glorious	מפואר	40מ+80פ+6ו+1א+200ר	327
(×3)	—	327 × 3	981
Thou	אתה	1א+400ת+5ה	406
Lover	אהובי	1א+5ה+6ו+2ב+10י	24
Supernal	עליון	70ע+30ל+10י+6ו+50ן	166
Self	עצמי	70ע+90צ+40מ+10י	210
Of myself	מעצמי	40מ+70ע+90צ+40מ+10י	250
TOTAL		981+406+24+166+210+250	2037

Reduction: 2+0+3+7 = 12 → 3

VII. Mispar Katan (Digit Reduction)

Word	Hechrechi	Reduced
מפואר 3×	981	9
אתה	406	1
אהובי	24	6
עליון	166	4
עצמי	210	3
מעצמי	250	7

Katan Sum: 9+1+6+4+3+7 = 30 → 3

VIII. Mispar Siduri (Ordinal)

Ordinal values: 22 (א) 1 ... (ב) 2 ... (ת)

Word	Ordinal Calculation	Sum
מפואר	מ13+פ17+ו6+א1+ר20	57
(3×)	57 × 3	171
אתה	א1+ת22+ה5	28
אהובי	א1+ה5+ו6+ב2+י10	24
עליון	ע16+ל12+י10+ו6+ן14	58
עצמי	ע16+צ18+מ13+י10	57
מעצמי	מ13+ע16+צ18+מ13+י10	70

Siduri Total: 171+28+24+58+57+70 = 408 → 12 → 3

IX. Milui (Spelling-Out)

Letter	Spelled	Value
א	אלף	111
ה	הא	6
ו	וו	12
ב	בית	412
י	יוד	20

Milui Total: 561 → 5+6+1 = 12 → 3

Repeated Milui on other key words preserves triadic collapse.

X. Atbash & Albam

Atbash transformations preserve total reduction to 3.

Albam substitutions alter surface values but not terminal collapse.

This confirms structural stability across classical transformations.

XI. Cross-System Convergence

Method	Final Reduction
English Payload	9
English Full Verse	3
Hebrew Hechrechi	3
Hebrew Katan	3
Hebrew Siduri	3
Hebrew Milui	3
Atbash (tested)	3
Albam (tested)	3

Independent systems → same terminal attractor

XII. Interpretation (Strictly Structural)

This convergence does not imply hidden prophecy or metaphysics. It demonstrates:

• Preservation of relational topology

• Language-independent reception invariance

• Constraint-driven meaning formation

• Stability of affective-structural imprint

The mathematics function as diagnostics of fidelity, not carriers of meaning.

XIII. Final Statement

Meaning is not transmitted. It is received.

Language changes symbols. The nervous system does not.

This verse behaves as a compression kernel whose structure survives translation, arithmetic, and symbolic transformation because it targets human reception constraints, not linguistic surface forms.

Technical Framework Overview
What This System Is — and Is Not

1. Core Claim

This work demonstrates that symbolic systems can be analyzed as reception-constrained information structures. Meaning is not treated as residing intrinsically within symbols. Meaning emerges at reception, shaped by shared cognitive and affective constraints. Structural invariants may persist across languages, alphabets, numeric encodings, and symbolic transformations.

This is a methodological claim.

2. System Components

A. Textual Kernel

A short, highly compressed symbolic passage (*Liber LXV* III:64) was treated as a constraint kernel rather than as narrative exposition.

B. Dual Analytic Tracks

The passage was processed through two independent systems.

Operational English letter arithmetic: A1Z26, Subject/Object/Predicate separation, arithmetic operations (addition, subtraction, multiplication, division), with reduction permitted at terminal stage to identify structural attractors.

Traditional Hebrew methods: Mispar Hechrechi (absolute value), Mispar Katan (reduction), Mispar Siduri (ordinal), Milui (spelling-out), Atbash (reversal cipher), Albam (half-alphabet substitution).

No procedural mixing of systems was permitted.

3. Function of Numerical Operations

The numerical procedures were diagnostic. They were used to test structural stability, invariance under transformation, and loss of fidelity under translation.

The numbers are not treated as carriers of hidden content. They function as indicators of whether relational structure persists across representational change. The role of invariance here is analogous to conserved quantities or symmetry conditions in formal systems.

4. Correspondence Constraints

Correspondence work was restricted to *Liber* 777 and canonical Golden Dawn attributions. No psychological synthesis, modern neuroscience overlay, or hybrid attribution systems were introduced under the label of 777. Correspondence tables functioned as fixed lookup matrices.

5. Information Model

The abstracted framework can be expressed as:

Input: Symbolic perturbation (text, word, phrase)
Medium: Human cognitive-affective system
Constraint: Neurobiological and emotional architecture
Process: Predictive integration and affective weighting
Output: Experienced meaning

Within this model, language, symbols, and numbers function as interfaces rather than intrinsic containers of meaning.

6. Excluded Claims

This work does not claim supernatural encoding, prophetic content, privileged revelation, scientific replacement, or metaphysical certainty.

It does not assert that gematria proves doctrinal propositions, that ancient texts encode modern science, or that numbers generate meaning independently of reception.

7. Demonstrated Outcomes

The analysis indicates that shared reception constraints operate independently of language. Structurally faithful translation preserves affective and relational coherence. Symbolic compression increases interpretive state-space. Mathematical operations can reveal structural invariants. Historical symbolic systems can be modeled as early cognitive technologies rather than as belief constructs.

8. Technical Summary

This framework treats symbolic texts as structured perturbations interacting with a human receiver. Multiple independent analytic systems—linguistic, numerical, and transformational—are applied to test relational invariance across representations. Where invariance persists, the result indicates stable reception dynamics rather than encoded metaphysical content.

The approach situates ancient symbolic practices within a cognitive and information-processing context compatible with predictive processing models and nonlinear systems theory, without requiring metaphysical premises.

Symbolic Compression as a Cognitive Operator

A Neurodynamic, Psychoneuroimmunological, and Nonlinear Systems Account

Abstract

Esoteric literature frequently describes certain texts as "magical technologies" capable of inducing non-ordinary cognition. This paper advances a non-metaphysical hypothesis: highly compressed symbolic texts, when repeatedly executed (read, recited, internalized), function as constraint-based cognitive operators. Specifically, such texts may (a) increase tolerance for prediction error, (b) promote metastable coordination among large-scale brain networks, (c) modulate attention and arousal indexed by oculomotor and pupillometric dynamics, and (d) indirectly influence immune and inflammatory processes through stress-regulatory pathways. The phrase "simultaneous poles of consciousness" is interpreted here as a metastable regime in which competing generative models remain co-activated without premature collapse.

1. Theoretical Frame:

Predictive Processing and the Free-Energy Principle

Contemporary models of cognition describe the brain as an inference engine minimizing prediction error through perception, action, and model revision (Friston, 2009, 2010). Under the Free-Energy Principle, internal models are continuously updated to reduce variational free energy (Friston, Kilner, & Harrison, 2006). Perception and action are therefore forms of constrained Bayesian inference.

Within this framework, a densely compressed symbolic text can be modeled as an engineered input distribution. Such input may destabilize low-level priors, delay semantic closure, and require iterative model revision. Repeated exposure under instruction (e.g., sustained rereading) may maintain model tension until higher-order integration reduces error. No metaphysical assumptions are required; the mechanism is inferential pressure under constraint.

2. Neurodynamics:

Multistability, Metastability, and Concurrent Model Activation

Coordination dynamics research demonstrates that brain activity often occupies regimes of multistability and metastability (Kelso, 2012; Tognoli & Kelso, 2014). Multistability refers to multiple available attractors; metastability describes partial integration and segregation without collapse into a single fixed point.

Operationally, "holding both poles at once" can be described as concurrent viability of competing generative models. Attention does not enforce immediate winner-take-all selection. Instead, cognition occupies a metastable manifold. This regime predicts increased paradox tolerance, reduced compulsive closure, and a higher likelihood of phase transitions experienced subjectively as insight.

3. Ocular Dynamics, Cadence, and Cognitive Effort

3.1 Pupillometry

Task-evoked pupil dilation is a robust index of cognitive effort and processing load (Kahneman & Beatty, 1966; Papesh et al., 2012). If symbolic compression increases inferential workload, measurable modulation of pupil diameter should occur. Such modulation reflects computational demand rather than mystical influence.

3.2 Cadence as Temporal Constraint

Prosodic structure and repetition-with-variation impose temporal regularity. Under predictive processing, regular timing reduces uncertainty in temporal prediction while preserving semantic ambiguity. This combination shifts inference upward in the model hierarchy. Cadence therefore functions as a constraint on attentional sampling and error resolution.

4. Psychoneuroimmunology: Indirect Pathways

Psychoneuroimmunology examines interactions among psychological state, neural regulation, endocrine signaling, and immune response (O'Connor et al., 2013; Ravi et al., 2021). Stress and inflammation are bidirectionally coupled.

The defensible claim is indirect: practices that alter stress regulation and autonomic balance may influence inflammatory tone. If symbolic compression practices modulate arousal, attentional control, or affective regulation, downstream immune effects are plausible within established PNI pathways. No direct symbolic encoding of physiology is implied.

5. Nonlinear Dynamics and State Space

Compact constraint systems can generate expansive state spaces. Nonlinear dynamics demonstrates how simple boundary conditions produce complex trajectories, bifurcations, and attractor landscapes (Strogatz, 2015).

A compressed symbolic kernel behaves less like semantic content and more like boundary conditions within cognitive state space. Repeated execution explores multiple trajectories constrained by the same structural rules. Complexity arises from iteration within fixed limits.

6. Quantum: Literal vs Analogical Use

6.1 Literal Domain

Quantum information science formalizes algorithms operating on quantum states (Nielsen & Chuang, 2010; Shor, 1997; Grover, 1997). These are physical systems with well-defined mathematical properties.

6.2 Analogical Use

Descriptions of "superposition" in symbolic cognition are analogical. Competing interpretations may coexist prior to collapse into a dominant narrative. Iterative constraint amplifies coherent pathways and dampens incoherent ones. This resembles interference and attractor selection in formal systems but does not imply quantum computation in neural tissue.

7. Testable Predictions

If symbolic compression functions as a cognitive operator under constraint, the following predictions are testable:

- Increased task-evoked pupil dilation during execution compared to matched prose controls
- Behavioral evidence of greater ambiguity tolerance and delayed semantic closure
- Neurodynamic signatures consistent with metastable coordination (e.g., transient synchrony patterns in EEG/MEG)
- Indirect improvements in stress markers and inflammatory proxies over time, mediated by autonomic regulation

These predictions are empirical and falsifiable. No metaphysical inference is required for their evaluation.

Reception-Centered Information Processing
Language-Invariant Meaning, Affective Imprints, and Neurodynamic Constraints

8. Reception Over Transmission

Classical communication models emphasize signal transmission: encoding, sending, and decoding information. However, contemporary evidence from neuroscience and cognitive science indicates that meaning is constructed at reception rather than transmitted as intrinsic semantic content. Incoming signals perturb internal generative models; meaning arises from how those perturbations are resolved (Friston, 2010).

Within predictive processing accounts, signals function as error-corrective inputs rather than semantic containers. Informational efficacy therefore depends on compatibility between message structure and the receiver's neurobiological constraints. The locus of meaning is reception dynamics, not signal form.

9. Language as Interface

9.1 Cross-Linguistic Affective Convergence

Emotionally salient directives (e.g., urgent prohibitions) reliably produce consistent behavioral and physiological responses across languages. These responses include boundary recognition, urgency detection, and action orientation. Such convergence suggests that affective intent is processed through evolutionarily conserved salience networks prior to full symbolic parsing (Pessoa, 2008).

Language, in this account, functions as an interface into affective and predictive systems. It does not carry intrinsic meaning independent of reception.

9.2 Evidence from Congenital Deafness

Individuals born deaf demonstrate fully developed reasoning, emotional nuance, and abstract planning. Neuroimaging shows that signed languages recruit core language networks also used in spoken language, with additional visual-spatial engagement (Neville et al., 1998; MacSweeney et al., 2008).

Cognition therefore does not depend on auditory phonology. Even in cases of early language deprivation, representational thought persists in non-verbal formats. These findings support the claim that structured experience precedes specific linguistic encoding.

10. Affective Imprints as Processing Invariants

10.1 Emotion as Processing Priority

Emotionally weighted stimuli are prioritized due to survival relevance. Core circuits—including amygdala, anterior cingulate cortex, insula, and autonomic regulators—show conserved activation patterns across individuals (LeDoux, 2012). These systems operate prior to and alongside symbolic interpretation.

Because affective processing is evolutionarily conserved, certain relational patterns (threat, enclosure, approach, separation) tend to retain impact across linguistic translation.

10.2 Structural Fidelity and Transformation

When relational topology is preserved across languages—such as containment, boundary, or opposition—symbolic transformations applied to those representations may preserve structural features. Convergence under such transformation reflects invariance rather than metaphysical equivalence.

Mathematical operations in this context function diagnostically. They test whether relational structure survives translation. They do not establish ontological identity.

11. Nonlinear Dynamics and Generative Compression

Highly compressed symbolic systems function as constraint kernels rather than extended narratives. Nonlinear dynamics demonstrates that small constraint sets can generate expansive state spaces and complex trajectories (Strogatz, 2015).

Repeated engagement with compressed symbolic material delays semantic closure and encourages metastable processing regimes. These regimes are characterized by concurrent model activation, delayed collapse into a single interpretation, and enhanced integrative transitions. Phenomenologically, this may correspond to the experience of holding multiple interpretations simultaneously.

12. Oculomotor and Temporal Dynamics

12.1 Pupillometry

Task-evoked pupil dilation reliably indexes cognitive effort (Kahneman & Beatty, 1966; Papesh et al., 2012). Texts that resist rapid semantic resolution increase inferential workload and should modulate pupil diameter accordingly. This reflects computational demand rather than hidden content transmission.

12.2 Cadence and Temporal Constraint

Rhythmic linguistic structure entrains neural timing mechanisms. Temporal predictability can coexist with semantic ambiguity, shifting processing toward higher-order integration. Cadence therefore shapes attentional and predictive cycles at reception.

13. Psychoneuroimmunological Considerations

Stress regulation significantly influences immune and inflammatory processes. Practices that enhance affect regulation and autonomic balance can indirectly modulate cortisol levels, inflammatory cytokines, and sympathetic-parasympathetic balance (O'Connor et al., 2013; Ravi et al., 2021).

Any physiological influence of symbolic practice would operate through regulatory pathways rather than direct symbolic encoding of biological parameters.

14. Clarifying Scope

14.1 Excluded Claims

This framework does not assert supernatural transmission, hidden linguistic messages, universal truths encoded in symbols, or quantum computation in neural tissue.

14.2 Positive Claims

It proposes that information is constrained by reception dynamics; that human neurobiology imposes invariant processing structures; that affectively salient relational patterns can persist across translation; and that mathematical operations can detect structural fidelity. Historical symbolic systems may be interpreted as early exploratory tools probing these constraints.

15. Synthesis

Across predictive processing, neurodynamics, linguistics, and nonlinear systems theory, convergent evidence supports a reception-centered account of meaning construction. Language, symbols, and numbers function as interfaces into a constrained biological system. Meaning emerges from structured perturbation interacting with that system.

This reframing situates symbolic traditions within a cognitive framework without requiring metaphysical assumptions.

APPENDIX B
On the Texts

Liber LXV vel Cordis Cincti Serpente

Liber LXV—*The Book of the Heart Girt with a Serpent*—is designated a Class A text within Thelema and was received by Aleister Crowley in 1907. Within the A∴A∴ classification system, Class A texts are described as inspired transmissions rather than conventional compositions and are not to be altered in wording or style. That status is internal to the tradition.

The book consists of five chapters structured as dialogues between an aspirant and the Holy Guardian Angel, a central figure in Thelemic practice. The language is highly symbolic and resistant to direct paraphrase. It presents images, paradoxes, and invocatory structures rather than systematic instruction. Interpretation varies with the state and context of the reader.

Chapter III served as the primary text for the work described in this book. It was memorized and recited as a repeated exercise. The analytical results presented here emerged from sustained engagement with that chapter.

Liber LXV functions less as discursive exposition and more as a compressed symbolic structure. Individual verses support multiple interpretive trajectories depending on the cognitive state of the reader. The text can therefore be modeled as a fixed input generating variable reception outcomes under constrained conditions.

All analyses in this book originate from that engagement.

The Holy Books of Thelema

Liber LXV forms part of a collection known as the Holy Books of Thelema, designated Class A texts transmitted between 1907 and 1911. First published in 1909 under the Greek title Θέλημα and later expanded, the collection contains writings Crowley presented as inspired or transmitted.

These texts are not systematic theology. They are symbolic compositions intended for ritual and contemplative use. Interpretation is not standardized; practitioners are expected to engage them directly rather than rely on authoritative commentary. This interpretive openness is structurally embedded in the system.

Central to the corpus is *Liber AL vel Legis* (*The Book of the Law*), received in Cairo in 1904. Crowley attributed its dictation to an entity named Aiwass. The text consists of three chapters, each associated with a symbolic deity: Nuit, Hadit, and Ra-Hoor-Khuit. Its structure is aphoristic and intentionally cryptic.

Liber AL explicitly discourages authoritative interpretation (III:42). The restriction functions as an internal doctrinal constraint. Meaning is framed as arising in reception rather than external commentary.

The broader corpus includes works such as Liber Liberi vel **Lapidis Lazuli, Liber Trigrammaton, Liber DCCCXIII vel Ararita, Liber B vel Magi, Liber Porta Lucis, Liber Stellae Rubeae, Liber Tzaddi vel Hamus Hermeticus, Liber Cheth vel Vallum Abiegni, Liber A'ash vel Capricorni Pneumatici, and Liber Tau vel Kabbalae Trium Literarum.** These texts employ dense symbolic, Qabalistic, alchemical, and initiatory language. They function operationally as ritual and contemplative material rather than as doctrinal systems.

In practice, the Holy Books operate as structured symbolic stimuli. Their use is experiential and iterative rather than exegetical. They are engaged rather than merely read.

Liber 777

Liber 777 vel Prolegomena Symbolica ad Systemam Sceptico-Mysticae Viae Explicandae, Fundamentum Hieroglyphicum Scientiae Mentis Humanae—commonly referred to as 777—was first published in 1909. It is a compilation of symbolic correspondences derived primarily from the Hermetic Order of the Golden Dawn and related Western esoteric systems.

The work is organized around the Qabalistic Tree of Life. Each Sephirah and path serves as a structural node linking multiple symbolic domains: Hebrew letters, divine names, angelic hierarchies, planetary and zodiacal attributions, Tarot trumps, alchemical processes, ritual implements, colors, and mythological figures. The Tree functions as the invariant relational framework.

The book consists primarily of numbered tables. Columns represent symbolic domains; rows align with Sephiroth or paths. The format assumes prior familiarity with Qabalistic structure. It is not designed for sequential reading but for reference and cross-mapping.

777 treats symbolic systems as parallel relational mappings rather than competing ontologies. Coherence is determined by structural alignment within the table, not by empirical validation.

Symbols are positioned as operators within consciousness rather than as carriers of intrinsic meaning.

Operationally, 777 functions as a coordination matrix. It enables symbolic substitution and relational comparison across domains. The practitioner performs synthesis; the book provides structure.

An implicit structural principle underlies the tables: distinct symbolic operations constrained by the same relational framework yield formally equivalent mappings. This principle governs the logic of correspondence. The book does not foreground it as a theorem, but its architecture assumes it.

In summary, Liber 777 is a structured symbolic interface. It provides a stable relational backbone for symbolic operations without requiring literal belief in any specific symbolic content.

The Equinox

The Equinox is a multi-volume periodical edited by Aleister Crowley. It combines archival publication, curriculum material, ritual texts, essays, translations, and literary work under a single editorial project. It was subtitled "The Review of Scientific Illuminism," which signals its stated intent: to present a record of methods, documents, and experiments rather than a devotional or doctrinal tract.

The publication assumes prior familiarity with ceremonial magic, Qabalah, Golden Dawn technical vocabulary, and related symbolic systems. Its layout is dense and frequently technical. This is consistent with its function as a repository for practitioners rather than an introductory resource. The editorial stance is often documentary: many materials are presented with minimal interpretive scaffolding.

The contents are heterogeneous by design. Volumes include rituals, instructional documents, commentaries, poetry, dramatic pieces, and source translations. This format reflects an assumption that magical work operates across multiple registers—technical, symbolic, affective, and aesthetic—and that documentation should preserve that range. The result is less a linear textbook than a reference environment.

Volume III is materially distinct in function from earlier issues. It consolidates technical and curricular content associated with the A∴A∴ framework. In that context, texts such as *Liber* 777 function as infrastructure: a correspondence matrix used to index and coordinate symbolic operations. The publication treats correspondences as operational mappings within a defined relational system rather than as claims about metaphysical truth.

A recurring methodological emphasis in *The Equinox* is disciplined practice: record-keeping, repeatability of method, and critical self-examination. Experiences are treated as reportable outcomes rather than as self-authenticating revelation. The standard is internal consistency and procedural control, not laboratory verification in the modern sense.

Magick in Theory and Practice

Magick in Theory and Practice forms the third part of Crowley's *Book Four* and functions as a technical exposition of method. The text defines magick as "the Science and Art of causing Change to occur in conformity with Will," framing it as a general theory of intentional action rather than a narrow instruction manual for ritual specialists. This definition deliberately collapses the boundary between ritual operation and ordinary agency.

The text is organized into conceptual chapters rather than progressive lessons. It presents postulates and theorems, then expands into topics such as ritual structure, the mechanics of invocation and evocation, symbolic weapons, and the relationship between microcosm and macrocosm. The pedagogy is iterative: concepts are introduced, revisited, and reframed rather than resolved in a single pass. The text assumes that comprehension increases through applied practice rather than through reading alone.

A central operational demand is experimental discipline. Crowley emphasizes record-keeping, self-observation, and analysis of success and failure. Failure is framed as misapplication or incomplete understanding of operational conditions rather than as moral defect. The model is lawful causation under imperfect knowledge.

Three interrelated ideas recur throughout the work. First, Will is treated as a governing principle distinguishable from impulse, habit, and social conditioning. Second, symbolism and correspondence function as operators within cognition rather than as supernatural mechanisms. Third, the microcosm-macrocosm analogy provides a structural rationale for treating internal change as formally related to external action. The text therefore functions as a framework for method rather than a catalogue of isolated techniques.

Closing

This framework is method-driven and auditable. No claim requires belief to be evaluated. Procedures can be repeated, and failures are informative. Convergences are treated as outcomes, not revelations.

"Love is the Law, Love under Will."

Journal Excerpt and Exam Materials

Frater Lachesis Peyton,

Journal - Dies Solis, Anno CXIII e.n.

Do what thou wilt shall be the whole of the Law.

Frater K,

I cannot thank you enough for the book recommendation; it is truly appreciated and has been more than helpful. Revisiting the yogic terms, and in such plain English, is elevating, as it gives me some fluidity while attempting to describe my thoughts on paper, and to another. Obviously the journal entries I have submitted thus far are lacking any true "magical" content. In other words, they are just my daily thoughts on paper. If nothing else it has captured my dross mood, as I feel I have been inundated by mundane reality, and yet mundane existence appears to be the bulk of life.

My current oath is to learn to enjoy the mundane and to give it new form by creating thought forms aligned with my efforts. Thought forms that can be utilized in a meditative sense must arise from actual conditions rather than imagined states. As an example, my battles with my x-wife and issues surrounding my daughter appear as the demons encroaching on my ability to be at peace, mentally speaking. They must be addressed directly, not symbolically. Therefore, if the Cup is understanding, then currently my cup is drained of the knowledge of how to defeat this enemy, and Chronos smiles while I hope for samadhi yet struggle through simple meditation.

I feel as though I have crossed some sort of starting line, though I hold no illusions that I will one day shoot fireballs from my hands or literally levitate. However, it is my hope to gain true magical abilities such as thought control and disciplined interior governance. As of late the ability to truly banish the negative forces in my life has been increasingly difficult. To become invisible to those forces would be priceless, but that invisibility must be earned through steadiness rather than fantasy. I feel as though I am wading through earth compressing me from all sides, and even so I continue to move forward.

I continue my studies and practices in earnest, though I am challenged in how to best express my experiences within a journal format. The act of writing itself becomes part of the discipline, not a report after the fact. I suspect that clarity of language reflects clarity of mind, and therefore this difficulty is instructional. Until further, I hope all is well with you. Love is the law, love under will.

Frater LP

A∴A∴ EXAM ADDENDUM

Dies Solis, Anno CXIII e.n.
Do what thou wilt shall be the whole of the Law.

1. Levithan, Abomination, and LA/AL

Based upon the readings, I have revisited what was written on pages 6 concerning "Levithan," "Abomination," and "Malkuth," and on pages 4-5 concerning LA/AL, seeking conceptual connections that tie into the sequence $1 + 2 + \ldots + 31 = 496$. At times in "Aiwass thinking," it feels as though I am Nuit, at other times Hadit, and then again the aspirant observing both. The aspirant appears at a loss, though perhaps this is one of those moments where the answer is present yet unseen. Each attempt to quantify, understand, or move beyond becomes an exercise in recognizing that the structure precedes the interpretation.

The strongest impression arising from rereading is that all resolves to one. If the original condition was unity, or perhaps nothing, then every iteration that follows may be understood as variation rather than departure. Under this reasoning, 496 and 1 may be considered structurally identical, the former simply an accumulation of units, the latter the seed. The idea that 1 alone is indistinguishable from nothing when no other observer is present underscores that designation itself requires relation. Thus the movement from unity to differentiation and back again describes a cycle rather than a linear expansion.

Turning to LA and AL, Aleph equals 1 and Lamed equals 30, and therefore LA equals 31. Adding the sequence from 1 to 31 yields 496, and the interplay between 31 and 496 becomes a field for structural examination rather than mystical speculation. If $31 + 31 = 62$ and $6 + 2 = 8$, then the reduction gestures toward infinity, not as metaphysics but as arithmetic collapse. Crowley himself remarks that many useless tricks may precede illumination, suggesting that the process of manipulation is itself instructive. The conclusion that God plus "not" yields totality is therefore a structural observation within the symbolic grid rather than a doctrinal proclamation.

Levithan, as an eight-letter form, evokes circularity and recurrence. The serpent consuming itself represents continuity rather than spectacle. In this frame, "Abomination" may signify inversion or contradiction that nevertheless participates in totality. Malkuth becomes the field of manifestation in which such inversions are perceived. The entire sequence thus reads as a demonstration that perspective shapes designation while structure remains consistent.

The movement through 1, 2, and 3 further illustrates this point. One names unity, two introduces polarity, and three permits relation between them. The Tarot correspondence between number and letter likewise reveals that designation and symbol are not identical. The Hierophant may be called fifth while bearing the sixth Hebrew letter, and that discrepancy is structural rather than erroneous. The arithmetic exercises demonstrate that perception, symbol, and reduction are interwoven.

Ultimately, the utility of these operations lies in disciplined attribution rather than ecstatic declaration. Fire, Water, Air, and Earth arise as stages of interpretation when structure is applied to lived experience. The circle closes not because meaning is imposed, but because recurrence is inherent in the system. In conclusion, all is one.

Love is the law, love under will.

Frater LaPa

References

Crowley, A. (1973). 777 *and other Qabalistic writings of Aleister Crowley*. Samuel Weiser. (Original work published 1909)

Crowley, A. (1986). *Liber LXV vel Corde Cincti Serpente*. Samuel Weiser. (Original work published 1907)

Friston, K. (2009). Predictive coding under the free-energy principle. *Philosophical Transactions of the Royal Society B: Biological Sciences, 364*(1521), 1211-1221.

Friston, K. (2010). The free-energy principle: A unified brain theory? *Nature Reviews Neuroscience, 11*(2), 127-138.

Friston, K., Kilner, J., & Harrison, L. (2006). A free energy principle for the brain. *Journal of Physiology-Paris, 100*(1-3), 70-87.

Kelso, J. A. S. (2012). Multistability and metastability: Understanding dynamic coordination in the brain. *Philosophical Transactions of the Royal Society B: Biological Sciences, 367*(1591), 906-918.

LeDoux, J. E. (2012). Rethinking the emotional brain. *Neuron, 73*(4), 653-676.

Pessoa, L. (2008). On the relationship between emotion and cognition. *Nature Reviews Neuroscience, 9*(2), 148-158.

Tognoli, E., & Kelso, J. A. S. (2014). The metastable brain. *Neuron, 81*(1), 35-48.

MacSweeney, M., Woll, B., Campbell, R., et al. (2008). The signing brain: The neurobiology of sign language. *Trends in Cognitive Sciences, 12*(11), 432-440.

Neville, H. J., et al. (1998). Cerebral organization for language in deaf and hearing subjects. *Proceedings of the National Academy of Sciences, 95*(3), 922-927.

O'Connor, T. G., Moynihan, J. A., & Caserta, M. T. (2013). Annual research review: The neuroinflammation hypothesis for stress-related psychiatric disorders. *Journal of Child Psychology and Psychiatry, 54*(4), 365-378.

Ravi, M., Miller, A. H., & Maes, M. (2021). The immunology of stress and depression. *Annual Review of Immunology, 39*, 799-825.

Strogatz, S. H. (2015). Nonlinear dynamics and chaos: With applications to physics, biology, chemistry, and engineering. Westview Press.

Kahneman, D., & Beatty, J. (1966). Pupil diameter and load on memory. *Science, 154*(3756), 1583-1585.

Papesh, M. H., et al. (2012). Cognitive effort reflected by pupil dilation. *Psychophysiology, 49*(10), 1304-1314.

Grover, L. K. (1997). Quantum mechanics helps in searching for a needle in a haystack. *Physical Review Letters, 79*(2), 325-328.

Nielsen, M. A., & Chuang, I. L. (2010). *Quantum computation and quantum information* (10th Anniversary ed.). Cambridge University Press.

Shor, P. W. (1997). Polynomial-time algorithms for prime factorization and discrete logarithms on a quantum computer. *SIAM Journal on Computing*, 26(5), 1484-1509.

www.ingramcontent.com/pod-product-compliance
Lightning Source LLC
Chambersburg PA
CBHW021205130626
46554CB00005B/1992